You, Me and Us
Exploring Our
Inner Realms
of Being

by

Lynda Ankrah

**Grosvenor House
Publishing Limited**

Lynda Ankrah is hereby identified as author of this
work in accordance with Section 77 of the Copyright, Designs
and Patents Act 1988

The book cover picture is copyright to Inmagine Corp LLC

This book is published by
Grosvenor House Publishing Ltd
28-30 High Street, Guildford, Surrey, GU1 3HY.
www.grosvenorhousepublishing.co.uk

A CIP record for this book
is available from the British Library

ISBN 1-905529-83-x

Acknowledgments

I would like to extend my love and gratitude to the following people.

My deepest love and thanks to my parents, Bernadette Livingstone and Frederick (Frank) Ankrah, who together co-created me and gave me life.

My heartfelt thanks to my husband, Andrew Forbes, for his many years of love, support, patience and encouragement (even though he thinks I'm a weirdo). Love ya, my Band of the Hus.

To my daughter Ishmel – Blessings from Ishtar (look to the Goddess for your guidance).

To my daughter Danielle – God has judged (look to your Guardian Angel for guidance).

To my grand-daughter Ja'Neale – the Wise Ones (the Grandmothers will guide you).

To Sue (Titania) Pixton for your friendship and encouragement. A warm welcome to baby James.

To William West, for all your encouragement, openness and acceptance (a true Quaker), even if I do think you're away with the fairies (in the nicest possible way), thanks chuck.

To Tony Atta – was it the Crusaders or Stanley Clarke? (Ask Mutley!!!)

I give thanks and homage to the creator and bow my head to the Goddess who bathed me in moonbeams and showered me with blessings.

And last but not least:

To my ancestors who guide me, bless me, hold me and live within me. I see your faces in the stars and hear your voices in the trees. I am loved, I am blessed.

Lynda Ankrah
Manchester, September 2006

Contents

CHAPTER ONE

We are all on a journey

We are all on a journey.

You may be aware of this; you may not be, at least not consciously.

Whatever the case, I would guess that recently you have been aware of a need within you to search for something, to look for answers to the many questions that life throws up.

Perhaps you are facing a decision to be made, a problem to be solved, a hurt to be healed.

I know this, because here you are, reading these words, holding this book.

Because the choice you have made to read these words is another step on your journey. Whether you now choose to continue reading is another step...

We have all been on this journey from before the day we were born into this world and will continue once we have left this world.

All the great spiritual teachers and leaders throughout history have talked about this journey. And countless millions of ordinary working people have based their lives on the awareness of this journey, in lands and cultures across the planet.

It is the journey of the soul, a spiritual journey, and this life we lead here on earth is only a small part of it. We are all travelling towards god/dess, towards enlightenment, heaven, nirvana, our future destiny, or whatever else we choose to call it.

Through this journey our spiritual selves should emerge, a bit like a beautiful butterfly coming out of a cocoon.

But wait a minute.

Before you go any further let me get a couple of things straight.

In the first place, this is not a book about some "supernatural" or "other world" experiences. The journey of the soul takes place here on earth, in our daily lives, and is very real. It's about the way we handle our relationships, how we interact with our jobs and careers, our families and friends, and also how we conduct ourselves when we have none of these things around us.

As our spiritual self emerges we become more empowered to learn the right lessons from our life experiences and to make the right choices, choices that will enhance and enrich our lives and the lives of those around us.

Our eyes may look to heaven, but let's keep our feet firmly on the ground!

The second thing I need to clarify is this: the journey of the soul that I'm talking about here has nothing to do with joining a church or belonging to a particular religion. People who belong to all the different religions and none, who follow all different beliefs or none, are all part of this journey, just by virtue of being alive. And this book is certainly not going to ask you to believe in any particular faith or religion.

The only faith I ask you to believe in is faith in yourself. Any other faith you wish to believe in is your personal choice.

This is not a book about waiting for someone else – no matter how "spiritual", "expert", "enlightened", "advanced", politically aware, articulate or knowledgeable they sound, or how many books they have read, or how many big words they can muster in a single sentence – to come along and be our saviour. Whatever the title a person may hold – "priest", "priestess", "vicar", "doctor", "imam", "rabbi", "professor" – they are still just people like you.

This is about YOU.

You, and the hidden priest/ess that lives deep within your own self. The spirit guide that lives within, to which we have given the name "intuition", who each and every one of us have met and at times allowed our self to be guided by - or at times have fallen out with.

I'm going to ask you to believe in yourself.

To trust your intuition.

I'm going to invite you to become more aware of the vast potential within you, and to develop your own ability to lead a fulfilling and positive life.

Hang on another minute, you might say. What gives you the right – or even the ability – to be our guide on this journey?

Well I'm certainly not holding myself up as an "expert"! I don't even consider myself a guide. I would call myself a facilitator, someone who wants to help by sharing experiences, not by telling you what to think or do.

In this book you'll hear a bit about my experiences of learning about the different energies – my own, and those of others around me.

3

Learning about these energies has enabled me to have a much deeper insight into myself and other people and our emotional, spiritual and physical well-being. It has enabled me to help others to develop greater awareness about themselves and to discover ways of becoming more self accepting.

But first I had to make my own journey towards a more self accepting way of being.

By sharing my experiences, I hope you will realise that you, too, are on a journey. It may not be the same journey as mine, but you may well find similarities, echoes, reflections of mine in yours, and yours in mine.

Sometimes we can feel stuck, or lost. Sometimes, for all sorts of reasons we don't feel ready to make this journey. Sometimes we don't even realise that we are on it!

Often our friends, our family, our workmates can't or won't help us along. Sadly, our nearest and dearest may even be the people who are standing in our way, stopping us from taking the next step. We somehow begin to feel exiled from ourselves.

After all, we live in a society where anything to do with soul or spirit is belittled or mocked. There are all sorts of distractions put in our path, including some very dangerous ones, like the addictions of drugs, gambling, alcohol, and abusive sex.

Faced with these obstacles, our journey turns into a struggle. Our dreams into nightmares. We experience a crisis, or what has come to be known as a spiritual emergency.

In this book I will touch on some of these experiences. Almost everything I say will be based on my own personal experiences of going through these struggles, as well as helping others through them.

We've all found ourselves in lonely, cold dark places, where it seems as if there is no way to get through.

But there is something deep within us that, if we are prepared to listen, calls us towards the light of self.

If you are ready, and this is the right time and place for you, read on.

This book is especially for you.

CHAPTER TWO

The First Step

Well, you've turned the page and you're still reading – it's now time for you to stop listening to me and tune in to yourself.

It's time to take the first step.

To do this, you'll need a bit of privacy and some peace and quiet. If you've not got these, then please close the book and don't start reading again until you've found somewhere where you can be alone with yourself for a few minutes.

Okay, sit quietly and take three deep breaths. Breathe in slowly and breathe out slowly... good.

Now, ask yourself honestly, is your life truly what you would want for yourself?

Take your time to think about this before reading on.

Are you happy? Are you hurting?

Again, take your time. Close your eyes for a minute or two and just think about the answers to these questions.

Just allow what ever is inside you to come up, be honest with yourself.

Do you feel you are heading in the right direction?

If not, why?

What do you feel is stopping you?

Again, close your eyes for a minute or two and think carefully about your answers.

Unless you choose otherwise, the answers are yours alone, not for anyone else's eyes, so you can be open and honest. Sometimes, because we are so used to thinking about other people, it can be difficult to focus on ourselves, so if answers don't come at once, don't worry, just wait for another quiet moment to yourself and try again.

Sometimes it can help to say the answers out aloud, or write them down on a piece of paper (you might well want to read it later!).

If you still feel a bit stuck, there are other ways of starting to reflect on yourself and your own journey.

For example, I teach a course called "Self Awareness and Personal Empowerment", during which I facilitate a group of people to explore their personal issues, and I usually start by asking them to think about their hopes and fears. They then share these with another member of the course.

You could make your own list of hopes and fears on a piece of paper, as another way of getting started. You could ask yourself "What are my hopes and fears for the next year, next month, next week even.

It's not, as they say, rocket science, but it is very valuable. Sometimes it's the simplest things that lead to the deepest revelations.

The main thing is to get beyond that part of ourselves which we show to people around us, and get to our inner self.

What do we really think about ourselves when we are

alone and nobody else is there to perform for? When we take off our masks, the ones we wear for the world, who is there?

Asking these questions of ourselves is a crucial part of our journey.

Now I obviously can't hear your answers, but let me guess at what your answers will show.

All of us have a mixture of things we see as good and bad in our lives, a mixture of happiness and sadness, pain and pleasure, hopes and fears.

It would be nice and simple if these things fell into neat groups, so we could for example say, "This person is bad and makes me unhappy, and this other person is good and makes me happy". Unfortunately, the good and the bad are most often all mixed up, often found in the same person, or the same experience.

It's time to look at the important question of *why* certain people are in our lives, *why* we have gone through the experiences we have.

I shouldn't have to tell you the answer, because you already know it! Yes, YOU have co-created all this mixture around you, through the choices and decisions you have made.

And once you have taken this huge step of embracing your own power, the most important questions in your life could start looking very different.

Instead of asking why things have happened to us, we have to ask why we have chosen to have these people in our lives, why we have chosen to go through the experiences we have had, why we have chosen to perform the roles we perform at work and with our families and friends.

The first step on our journey is to take full responsibility for ourselves. It's a big step, yes, but my goodness it's empowering!

Before going any further, try it out by looking back on one or two experiences you have found painful.

For example, instead of asking "Why did I have to break my leg that time?" and "why do things like this always happen to me?" try and think about what you learned from the experience about yourself and about other's.

You may find that you learned a lot about the kindness of others, or realised who your friends really were during that time of crisis in your life, or learned to be more appreciative of the joy of having two working legs!

Instead of asking, "Why did I have to go through such a difficult love affair or relationship?" ask: "Why did I choose to go through such a difficult relationship? Why did I choose the person I did and how did I contribute to the situation? What did I learn about my own behaviour?"

And so on.

In your mind's eye, take some time to go back through your life from the perspective of having chosen each step of your journey, in your adult life

By taking full responsibility for yourself, by asking questions from a position of responsibility for your own experiences, you'll find you learn a great deal about your own self and your relationship with those around you.

You and Others

It's time to forget about the idea that each person is a little island, completely disconnected from everyone else. Each "self" is not a separate thing.

Just the opposite. Each "self" is in fact deeply connected to each other "self", rather like each socket is part of an electrical circuit.

Picture the self as part of a universal energy system.

Think of it as that place where the creator in you recognises the creator in me.

It's also that place where the destroyer in you recognises the destroyer in me.

Oh, yes we all have different aspects of self that we give birth to. That's why our lives are made up of such contrasting and contradictory manifestations.

Yes, we're all mixed up, as the song goes!

When we show someone having a thought in cartoons we usually draw a lighted bulb hovering above the person's head. This is not because a lighted bulb actually appears! It is a metaphor, because no one actually knows what a thought looks like, but it is an image that is actually very close to the truth.

Science tells us that our brain waves are electrical pulses of energy. These electrical currents can be detected in each and every living creature on the planet. So each time we think or feel something a pulse of energy is released into the universe.

These pulses connect to and meet with other energy impulses of thought and they all form a universal soup of collective energy that has been called the collective consciousness. We can imagine this as a collection of thoughts and memories, a bit like a giant library from which we can receive information.

That's why we are never truly alone. Consciously or unconsciously we are surrounded by this living energy, and tuning in to this energy is an important part of becoming aware of our selves and our true potential.

Each time someone in our environment thinks or feels something we can pick up this energy pulse, if we allow ourselves to be sensitive to it.

Most important of all, is our natural ability to change the world around us through the energy we radiate.

Our energy intentions are at play every second. That's why it's so important to take responsibility for our own thoughts. As the saying goes, "be careful of what you wish for, you might just get it"!

If we have the intention and the belief we can create miracles around us and sometimes the miracles are so small and appear so ordinary that we can fail to see them and dismiss them as nothing more than "good luck" or a fluke or a coincidence.

No, these are not some accidental events; these are wishes that you have manifested into being by your intent.

Think again about the answers you gave to the questions I asked at the beginning of this chapter. How many of them would you acknowledge as being your wishes? How many of them – even the ones that appear to be giving you negative experiences – are actually the manifestation of your intentions? How many have you helped to create into your own reality?

This may be difficult to accept at first, because we are so used to denying our own inner power. But before you turn away from the idea, answer a few more questions for me.

Have you ever been thinking about someone you haven't seen for a while and all of a sudden you just know that you will see them? (Lovers often experience this as their energy is pretty well tuned in to each other.) No sooner have you had the thought than suddenly they just appear? "Oh my goodness!" you say in astonishment. "I was just thinking about you!"

Hello! Are you psychic?

Has the phone rung or the door been knocked and you know who it is before you pick up the phone or open the door? "I just knew it was you," we tell the other person.

Hello! Are you psychic?

Have you ever known what someone was going to say before they said it? "Oh," we say, "I knew you were going to say that!"

Hello…!?

Have you ever done some thing or gone somewhere that you knew deep down felt wrong and then in the light of experience found yourself afterwards saying I knew I shouldn't have …

Hello…!?

So you see there is really nothing to it! It's your naturally "psychic" self working inside you, just waiting for you to turn on and tune in. All you have to do is believe it is there and trust yourself enough to allow it to emerge.

It's a gift that belongs to all of us. It's a way of life in some parts of the world and 100 percent natural.

So forget about Mystic Mog or what ever her name is and tune into your own naturally "psychic" self.

In fact, what some call "psychic ability" is simply the ability to connect with the energy that is inside us. We don't have to be special to tap into the life force pulsating through us. The fact that we are alive makes us special.

It is our birth right and a matter of free will on our part to choose whether to receive or to connect to our true inner self.

One thing is certain, though. If we choose to make the

connection to our deeper self we will begin to solve and heal the frustrations, sadnesses and hurts that can burden our lives.

Finding Support Around Us

Now you've taken the first step you may be champing at the bit to get on to the next step, and the next.

But hold on just a while. The journey you are taking is not a simple, straightforward march from 'A' to 'B'. It's more like pottering around the garden – you often get the most done when you go back over familiar ground, or even go round in a circle!

So take a bit more time at this stage to repeat the first step. Ask yourself again what you are trying to achieve. What are the issues in your life that you wish to tackle, and what are your goals, your wishes, your dreams?

It may well be worth taking this up as a regular habit – spending a few minutes of quiet, private time each day or week or each month to think about where you are and where you want to be in your life. The answers to your questions may change, depending on what is happening in your life and within yourself.

It's called meditation, and, no, you don't have to be a Buddhist, sit with your legs around your neck, or chant rhymes in foreign tongues to meditate perfectly success-fully (though I'm not stopping you if that's what you want to do!). Like many of the most important things in life, it's a simple procedure, which just requires a few minutes of time to yourself.

For example, try simply going to a park near to you and reflecting on your life as you walk through trees and plants. This is what is known as a walking meditation, and is particularly good for those who find it difficult to sit still for long periods of time.

Nature is wonderful for reflective meditation, but don't take my word for it, just try it!

It's one of many things we can do which begin to provide us with practical support in beginning our journey. Nature provides us with all sorts of inexpensive, ready-to-hand resources which can help us. There are now hundreds of shops and internet sites which can point us towards these resources, but to be honest, a lot of them are right there in front of us!

All of them work by either changing the energy around us, or by changing the energy within us. Either way, the one affects the other.

To change the energy around you, bring natural things into your environment. Surround yourself with plants, flowers, dried wood, stones, sea shells, crystals, or objects made from these things. Listen to them, touch them, feel their energy.

Nature is full of natural bling – I call it the bling of the soul!

Use colours found in nature in your home decoration and your choice of furniture.

I could carry on, but I'm sure you get the idea! Anyway, there are hundreds of books, magazines, websites and courses which will give you thousands of good ideas about these basic sources of support; you don't need me to tell you what you can find out so easily.

Don't underestimate the importance of these simple resources. Just because they may seem "cheap" compared to designer bling, don't fall into the trap of thinking they're low in value.

Oh, and one important thing to remember: nothing is for free. If you take something, no matter how small, from Mother Nature, you need to first of all ask your inner self, "Is it OK to take this?", and wait for an answer. You will know if it right or not.

Nature is not dead. Nature is alive and communicates with us all the time if we care to listen.

For example, if we are trying to pick up a stone or a piece of wood that has attracted our attention and we find it is difficult to pick up or feels slightly stuck, then you have a clear message: No! Leave it be.

Even when we sense that the answer is "yes", and it's OK to take something, it's good to always give something back in exchange. This could be a crystal, a coin, or even a prayer. All that's needed is some form of energy exchange – even some bread for the birds is fine with Mother Nature.

And always remember to say thank you.

As you go further along your journey you're going to appreciate all the help you can get, because working with energy – especially the negative energy that keeps us from fulfilling our purpose – is a difficult and demanding task.

The next step is to explore more deeply the way in which the energies around us affect our lives.

CHAPTER THREE

Energy Is All Around Us

Have you ever been in the company of someone who was being really negative and sorry for themselves?

No matter what you suggest there is always a reason why they can't do it or why it wouldn't work. "Yes, but..." is usually their favourite word and it does not matter how much they profess to wanting to change, move on, get out of the situation, there is always a "yes, but..."

This tiny, tiny phrase is a very powerful magic charm, a way of cancelling out every opportunity you have given them to get out of the situation they so ardently argue they want to escape from.

Let's face it, even if you offered them a whole stack of "Get out of jail free" cards they would still choose to stay, chanting their mantra of "yes, but"!

Do you remember how after being with them for a while you felt drained tired and exasperated? Well, you had just been zapped of your energy!

I call this type of person a "Victim Leech". The victim leech attaches him or herself to you and begins a slow process of draining your energy. They do this by making you believe you are really important to them. By getting you to believe that, with your help, they are just about to have a breakthrough or an insight into their situation. You tend to work very hard with this particular person because they seem so helpless and always have a good old sob story to intrigue you with, but somehow that breakthrough never comes.

You will notice at times they will profess to "feeling a bit better now" -never just "better", always "a bit better" - and off they'll go, while you are left feeling weak, drained, tired, ill and down.

If this situation rings a bell with you, you've already had an experience of the sort of problems we all face on an energy level. You, my friend, have had your energy drained by a victim leech.

For them, it's always, always someone else's fault. Never have they had a part to play in any of it, and if you dare to suggest such a thing, or to point out the part they have played in creating their own situation they are gone! Gone, that is, after telling you how wrong you are and how you kicked them when they were down and how "you never help them".

Victim leeches are the sort of people who will slowly suck and feed off your energy for as long as you allow them to. With them, there is always a problem and never a solution, so you feel as if you are being held to ransom emotionally. Eventually, for your own good, you have to peel yourself away from them.

When you start to become aware of this kind of energy drain it's not generally a good idea to confront the person; it's often best to make your excuses and withdraw gracefully. Remember, this person is not interested in acknowledging the effect of their own behaviour on you. They perceive challenge as attack, and view anyone who challenges them as being aggressive towards them. If you confront them they will simply see you as another person who has been mean and horrible to them, and move on to their next unsuspecting victim.

Working with this sort of energy takes a lot of time and skill, and unless you've got energy to spare, this person is best kept at arm's length. Respect them as a person with feelings, and offer what friendship you can, but don't allow them to suck you in or drain you.

The victim leech is one of many types of negative energy manifestation that can directly affect your health and prevent you from achieving your own goals in life.

And by the way – how active is your own inner victim leech? When does this creature show up inside you?

Let's not spend too much time looking at others without looking more closely at ourselves.

In fact, working with your own energy is your first priority. First and foremost, you need to develop your own awareness and empower your own self.

We have already seen how the energies created by our inner thoughts and intentions are just like electricity – they may not be visible to us but they exist all around us and have always done so. Just as there are invisible forms of physical energy – like electricity, magnetism and nuclear radiation – so there are invisible forms of psychic or spiritual energy.

While we usually can't see these directly, we can get to know them through observing their effects on people around us – again, just like many forms of physical energy.

Put this book down, now. Look around you, and become aware of your immediate surroundings. Look at the objects and colours around you. What about the people around you – what energy are they radiating, or exchanging. Is it angry energy, sad energy, resentful, happy?

Spend some time in the next few days and weeks observing the people around you. Think about relationships you have had, or may still be having. See if you can begin to recognise the positive and negative energies that flow between all of us as we interact in our daily life.

Understanding Energy

But where do these energies come from? And what determines whether they take negative or positive forms?

It is the energy of intent that gives birth to negative or positive energy manifestations. It is the energy of intent that brings forth the co-creation of harmonious or destructive entities.

To understand this better, let's take the example of music. On a physical level, as we know, music is created through making vibrations in the air. It is a form of sound energy.

But skilled composers and musicians know exactly what they are doing when they are creating with the vibrational octaves of music, and it is not about creating sound waves! It's about using energy to communicate at a deep energy level. That's why music can stir such strong feeling within us, that's why people have created music therapy and composed meditational music.

All of these people share a common purpose; an intention to create a state of being for you through sound energy.

Emotions.

E – motions.

Energy in motion.

Music is a living entity that we call into being; if it wasn't, it would not affect us at such a deep, organic level of being. Advertising uses music very successfully to speak to your subconscious. People talk about the shamans of "primitive" tribes; what do you think the shamanic tribesmen of advertising are doing? Summoning up a particular energy state for you to go shopping and spending beyond your means! Oooh! How primitive!

If it did not work do you really think these people would spend millions of pounds on advertising and be paying pop groups and other musicians thousands of pounds to allow their tunes to be projected around the world? Why is music played in shopping precincts and stores, if not to entrance you in the shop's entrance?

Music can be used to create harmony or feed aggression. It can inspire people to love or to war; to commit crimes, or to support good causes.

It's all a matter of the intent in the mind and heart of the creator of the music.

In just the same way, our own intentions manifest themselves in the energy forms around us. Yes, we are all creators of something.

For some of these energies, we can take sole responsibility. For many of them, however, we are partly responsible, sometimes without being fully aware of what we are doing.

We are for the most part walking around unconscious.

All of us are involved in group activities in which we choose to put our individual energy into a pool of collective energy, sometimes with a small group of family or friends, sometimes with a large group in a crowd, sometimes in vast collective pools of consciousness involving thousands or even millions of others.

We call these activities traditions, cultural practices, rituals.

The rituals of we who live in the technological world are often ignored and go unlabeled and unquestioned, while the rituals of others are queried and belittled; one is called "civilised" and the other is called "primitive".

Documentaries and books describe the face painting of native people going in to battle, or those performing rites of passage rituals, or fertility rituals, or rituals of marriage or coming of age, as superstitious, primitive practices.

What then of the primitive superstitious practices of tribal gathering and tribal face painting of English people before they go to a symbolic war against another tribe while chanting, clapping hands together and banging feet on the floor to create a drum like sound? It's called a football match!

It's designed to create a mass trance state of oneness and unity between the people present. It is almost a spiritual state and is the closest some people ever get to experiencing a collective purpose. This is no different to shamans chanting and calling for the wellbeing of a people, banging drums to create wellbeing and to banish negative energy.

Forgive me for not seeing the difference between the two as being anything to do with one being civilised and the other primitive. They are both ritualistic trance-inducing cultural practices, calling a collective oneness into being. They are both designed consciously to call certain energies into being.

The key is the intent behind them.

The shamans know what they are doing; they are using a wisdom that has been around for thousands of years, a wisdom designed to keep a community healthy and in balance.

So what then are we calling into being for our young people, not to mention what entities are we summoning up through our own thought forms and birthing in to existence?

What are we to make of the modern tribal rituals of the technological world that we see every week on our television screens, the rituals of football, music, going out clubbing, drinking in all-day bars and fighting in town centre streets?

And what part – consciously or unconsciously – are we playing in helping these energies manifest themselves in our lives and the lives of those around us?

See how far this next step has taken you? Once you begin to realise the nature of the energy within you and around you, and to realise how your own personal intentions – your wishes, curses, fears, hopes, dreams, nightmares, prayers – join with those of people around you, you have begun to embrace a great responsibility.

As I said earlier, you have the ability within you to be both creator and destroyer, of your own life, and the lives of those around you.

If this is too much for you, it's time to close this book. If you've bought it, then please pass it on to someone else. If you've borrowed it, from a library or a friend, take it back – someone else is waiting to read it…

Whatever you do, don't read any more pages unless you are prepared to take responsibility for the power that is within you.

You see, it's not what you may discover in this little book that's important; it's what the book may discover in you.

By reading on, you really could change your life.

CHAPTER FOUR

A Little Bit About My Journey

Let me take some time now to tell you a little bit about my own journey, and how I came to learn about the potential within myself.

I have been working with people for the past 25 years in numerous settings: youth work, play work, prison, rape crisis centre, counselling, teaching and running courses in further and adult education colleges and at a Women's Centre.

I can now look back and realise that the nature of my work means I have been steeped in people and their energy throughout my adult life. The intensity of this work, often involving forming close relationships with people in crisis, sometimes threatened to overwhelm me, and I would need to take time out. Again, I didn't understand this fully at the time, and simply considered myself exhausted, or ill, but now realise that I had to take myself out of circulation to cleanse and replenish my own energy field.

It was many years before I came to understand what it was I was experiencing. Sometimes I would be around people and begin to feel the energy formation around them. It wasn't something I could put in to words; it was a strong feeling, an inner sensation, something for which I didn't have a vocabulary.

During my younger years growing up I had always been able to sense the connections between things, events, people, behaviours and the effect on the planet. I can remember being told on numerous occasions to stop looking for things that don't exist and reading too much into things.

Through out my teenage years I became quite rebellious, especially at school. I would question teachers and challenge their attitude, and as a result I was labelled cheeky and disruptive. I also gave many of my fellow pupils a hard time. I wanted so desperately to fit in, but just didn't know how to. I didn't do at all well at school, and was written off by many – including many members of my own family – as someone who would never be able to make a success of life.

I was unable to explain or to articulate my experiences to the people around me. In the modern world we struggle to find a language to talk about things of the spirit, and so it often seems easier to say nothing at all.

Interestingly enough I remember at a particular point in my life -somewhere around my teens and twenties - trying to clumsily, inarticulately and unconfidently explain that I didn't think you could understand politics without spirituality because politics and spirituality are interconnected.

I can remember all too well the icy glare of the person's response to that idea, and the dismissal of my opinion as if I was thick, naïve, stupid and almost certainly unintelligent! So while around certain people I developed a habit of not speaking, which they in their arrogance and narrow mindedness took to mean I had no opinion. "Just a pretty face" was a comment I heard more than once: how arrogant and derogatory can you get!

It was at these times I would doubt myself and start to think there was something radically wrong with me for thinking the way I did.

By now I had learned to be very selective about whom I spoke to about these experiences. This was reinforced when I underwent a period in my life when I seemed to be having what is commonly known in this culture as "a psychotic episode", complete with visions, voices, seeing energy forming as glowing light around people and trees. I remember one winter's day when it started snowing being all of a sudden able to see the structural energy patterning of a single snowflake, just with my naked eye, without the aid of a microscope.

I tried to speak about my experiences to friends and family, just as I had when I was a child, but quickly realised this was not only seen by others as "not okay", but that it was positively dangerous for me to do so. The more I said the more people began to act as if there was something drastically wrong with me - especially my mother, who for years could only feel exasperation around me and would constantly tell me not to talk about things.

Needless to say I totally tried to suppress that side of me that I now realise was somehow naturally "tuned in" to the inner realm of living energy. I locked it away as much as I could, and stopped talking about those experiences altogether.

I myself became afraid of me.

These experiences had such a profound effect on me I became very cautious around people for fear of being pathologised – labelled as ill or sick or insane. I kept people at a safe but lonely distance for fear of them seeing me as strange and not well.

For those who, for whatever reason, are born sensitive or become sensitive to the invisible energies around us and within us, life can be difficult and lonely. Unless we are lucky enough to be born into a culture or family that acknowledges the invisible world, or find people near us who are accepting and open-minded, life can be a struggle.

∽

I was never part of the "in crowd". Or the politically "sorted" brigade. Nobody ever asked my opinion or bothered with what I thought, mainly because everyone thought I was an air-head without an opinion! Everyone, that is, except one woman who I had known most of my life and called Aunty.

Aunty would often ask me about what I believed and why – at the time I thought of her as interrogating me. She was a very straightforward and opinionated woman and at times I was intimidated by her, yet she was the only one at that time who ever showed a genuine interest in my inner thoughts.

Interestingly enough just before she passed away I would visit Aunty and do some healing and crystal work with her. This was not to heal her from her illness nor with some misguided notion of "saving" her from her inevitable journey to the realm of ancestor-hood. This was so she could begin to embrace her journey to the ancestors and feel some sense of energy, relief, acceptance and acknowledgement of death as part of the same intercon-nectedness to life, in much the same way I had seen the interconnectedness of politics and spirituality and the web of all life that connects the universe in all its forms and expressions.

Our time together was an experience of politics and spirituality in action.

At this time she and I revisited the conversations we had had years earlier, when I had talked hesitatingly to her about my beliefs about spirituality and its interconnectedness to politics and why I believed one could not exist without the other. The difference now was that I was much more confident in my own beliefs and trusted my experiences and perceptions a lot more.

I was much more comfortable within myself by this time.

We both really looked forward to our meetings and I was absolutely bowled over that this politically strong and opinionated woman could possibly be interested in what I had to say and how I saw the world.

One day I went round as usual, but something magical happened. Aunty presented me with a brown rag doll she had had made for me.

I was simply flabbergasted, because as a child the two things I had always wanted were a wagon train with horses, and a brown rag doll which I had seen in the window of the local toy shop when I was eight years old.

I never got either of these! I was told that wagon trains were for boys, not girls.

As for my brown rag doll; instead I got a white Tressy doll, a sort of early version of the Barbie doll, which I remember had a big hole in the top of its head from which you pulled a tuft of hair so you could comb her long blonde hair. I was told I should be grateful because all the other kids had Tressy.

But I didn't want what all the other kids had; I wanted a brown rag doll! I was a girl with brown skin and curly dark hair. It was very important for me to have a brown rag doll to identify with. I could not express that nor did I consciously know that as a young child; all I knew was I desperately wanted this doll I had seen and was extremely distressed that I never got her. I hated Tressy and cut all her hair off, leading my parents to call me wicked and ungrateful!

I hadn't discussed any of this with Aunty. Indeed I myself had forgotten all about it until the day she presented me with the doll (it's amazing what we suppress and what comes up from the subconscious).

So when I was finally presented with a beautiful brown rag doll it was very, very meaningful for me. Aunty had unconsciously given me a very significant and symbolic gift from one soul to another. It has a butterfly embroidered on the corner of its apron; butterflies are symbolic of transformation and an expression of the soul.

To this day I quite often feel connected to Aunty through this magical gift she gave me, the doll I had always wanted, but had forgotten.

The brown rag doll has pride of place in my bedroom. It serves to remind me that it's never too late to realise your dreams and goals and that gifts of the soul can come along when you least expect them.

The brown rag doll symbolises the real me, my aspiration – frustrated throughout childhood - to connect to my true self, and be embraced and accepted for my true nature.

I was ashamed of some of the things I did in my child-hood and teenage years - my wild, and often hurtful angry, dysfunctional behaviour led me to make all sorts of mistakes which I am not proud of – but I can now see much of this behaviour as a desperate response to the lack of care and understanding I was surrounded with. Children have wisdom they cannot articulate.

Aunty's gift represents a turning point. It helped me to stop focussing on everything that I had done wrong in my life, and embrace myself for who I am. And to stop being so controlled by other peoples judgements and opinions of me. It was time I saw and embraced the goodness in me.

Having heard a part of my story, take some time once again to reflect, just a few minutes to yourself.

This time think back over your early years and see if you can remember times when you felt you were in touch with the invisible energy world.

This could have been, for example, a time when you felt connected to animals or birds or felt you saw human shapes, angels or pictures in the clouds. Perhaps you felt as if you were connected to the natural world around you, or you may have been taken to places and felt you had been there before because it felt so familiar to you .Or you may have found yourself collecting stones or seashells because you felt attracted to them, long before you knew about crystals for healing.

Some of you may have felt connected with "imaginary friends", invisible friends you played with and talked to quite naturally. Or you may have sensed a presence in the room with you, and been aware of a whole other world next door to ours.

The adults around you may have rationalised this as a child's "over-active" imagination, or as some sort of play-acting fantasy. This may have made it difficult

for you to accept and embrace your own intuitive self –
but your intuition is still there, if you choose to acknowledge it.

Now think about gifts you may have received, which
may have been particularly important in your development. Who was the giver? Remember, this gift may not
have been an object like my doll, but something someone
did for you. Did you feel that the gift was a manifestation
of a hope or a wish that was dear to your heart?

Finally, reflect on mistakes you may have made –
poor behaviour that may have upset, frightened or
insulted others – and see if you can see them as the manifestation of a frustrated hope, wish or aspiration or a
response to your own pain.

But don't spend more than a few minutes on this.
Don't dwell on your mistakes.

No matter what mistakes you have made in your life
that's all they are, mistakes you have made.

We are not our mistakes.

We are divine beings in a state of becoming and we
have a right to be allowed to move on from our mistakes.

If people won't let us move on in their mind then its
time for us to let go of those people and give ourselves
time to grow and permission to move on, do better and
become all that we can.

Those people we think have all the answers and
are so important, yes, they do have some of the knowledge, information and answers, but you know what?
They don't have all of them! They are only people with
some knowledge. And remember they too have their
own dysfunctional self. You yourself also have many
answers.

Divine knowledge, information, inspiration, lives inside us, each one of us, and is not reserved for the most popular or to the "in crowd".

Divine knowledge and intelligence, whether emotional, political or spiritual, lives inside every one of us.

Yes, we all have a direct line to the creator, regardless of race, class, colour, culture, religious orientation, or whatever spiritual path you follow or not.

It is the universal right of each and every living soul, since each individual soul is connected to the soul of the world.

Therefore you don't have to experience god/dess through a third party!

The source lives inside you. It is not out there somewhere in the pages of a book.

It's not in this book, nor any other book, be it the Bible, the Koran, the Qaballa, the Torah. Yes, they can all bear expression from the creator but they in themselves are not the creator; they are not the source itself, only an expression of the source.

The source lived long before any book ever did. The book is made by the intention of the spirit which moves the hand that writes it.

Oh, and by the way, dear reader, we're coming back to you again. I hope you have found the part of my life story I have shared interesting, and you now feel you know a little bit more about the author of this particular piece of writing.

Because the meaning of this book is ultimately all to do with the relationship between me and you, as co-creators.

This book, any book, is infused with the energy and life force of its creator, who breathes life into the meaning of the book and births an intention into being.

That's what I'm doing.

That intent in turn resonates (or not) with the energy, life force and intent of the recipient.

You.

Now we know each other better, let's continue our journey together.

CHAPTER FIVE

Getting in Touch With the Many Yous

It's now time to be introduced to your self properly.

Or, to be more precise, to be introduced to your selves.

Do you remember that I mentioned earlier on the different aspects of self that we give birth to? Well, I wasn't joking! We may have a single physical body, a single face, a single legal identity, but we are in fact made up of many different, overlapping, interconnecting selves. We are indeed multiple personalities.

We have been conditioned to think of things as solid objects, independent from other objects and self-contained. We also tend to think of ourselves and those people around us in the same way, as self-contained, separate beings who interact with each other.

Nothing could be further from the truth. It's time to stop talking about the self as if it were a frozen, congealed entity.

The self is not solid, it's fluid.

It doesn't stand still; it's in constant motion.

Just like fire, wind and water, and – as we now know – the earth herself.

The self is a set of energies, moving through time and space.

Many wise traditions compare the self to light, and talk of us as beings made of light. Those who choose to work with people and their energies as healers have adopted the name "light workers".

There are many different ways of describing the life force that inhabits your body, that animates you, that stirs your heart and mind to create thoughts and feelings, that uses symbols and sounds to express those ideas and emotions, that in short makes you you.

And that life force takes on many different forms in your life: these are your different selves.

This is a familiar idea to us when we look at nature. Take water, one of the essential ingredients of life.

Water is still (for the scientifically minded among us) H_2O no matter how it is arranged, whether it is in the form of ice - square or in cubes - in hailstones, small or large balls, fluid, droplets as in rain, flowing as in a river, trickling as in a stream, waves as in the ocean, steam as in a kettle, shower or sauna, sweat, urine, tears - it does not matter what arrangement it's in, the essence is still water: it's from the same source.

It's the same with your inner self. You are made of the same essential life energy, but depending on the environment you find yourself in, and the way other energies affect you, this life energy can manifest itself in a whole variety of ways. Just as water does you may become rigid and closed, (frozen) or open and creative (fluid).

If you're feeling confident, and don't mind involving others at this stage in your journey, you can raise your awareness of your different selves by asking people around you how they would describe you. Try, for example, asking family members, friends, neighbours, people at work, people you know through leisure pursuits - as many different people as you can – to tell you three things about you; two things they like about you and one thing they're not so keen on. The answers can be surprising, amusing, even disturbing, but they should cast light on the different aspects of your self that others see.

This is where the opportunity to explore these issues together as a group is so valuable and empowering. Working with others in a supportive environment can be a very powerful way of opening up your inner selves.

At the source of everything is your divine self, that deep, inner self which, if you let it, will guide you along the path of your life, your spiritual journey.

Hopefully you have begun to embrace some of the ways I have suggested you might use to gain more insight into your inner self. As I've said, it doesn't matter what belief system or religion you may have. It's all about how you can help yourself by manifesting energy from your inner self for your highest good.

Embracing your divine self is not about being perfect and never making mistakes. It's about making a commitment to working with our whole self including our dysfunctional self, and accepting that we all make bad choices and wrong decisions.

It's about being human and divine all at the same time. It's about accepting the many aspects that live within the universal soul of the self.

In fact, being able to really embrace our divine self is the goal of the journey we are all on. We are on a journey precisely because we haven't yet learned everything we need to know to be able to connect to this universal energy.

The lessons we have to learn are not some weird and wonderful fairy-tale challenges involving dragons and maidens; fairy stories are invaluable because they help us understand the moral and spiritual meaning of our journey, but our task is to learn from the real-life challenges that face us week in, week out.

Those challenges involve those other aspects of our self which attach us to the collective consciousness which is the society around us.

Too often, this is as much a collective madness as anything else, which is why so many of us struggle to achieve the awareness necessary to get in touch with our deeper selves.

We need to understand and embrace our natural self.

Which, by the way, has nothing to do with the word "normal"! What is

"normal" for you might be destructive for me and vice versa.

I am talking about the aspect of self which connects to the natural world around us, and draws nurture from the generous gifts of mother nature.

Too often, we have chosen to try and control and dominate nature, rather than work along with her, and we have therefore become disconnected from our natural selves.

We need to understand and embrace our sexual self.

This aspect of the self is where the fundamental energies of the masculine and feminine should find their balance.

Too often, these energies are completely out of

balance, and we can fall into self-destructive patterns of perverse and abusive behaviour.

We need to understand and embrace our cultural self.

This aspect of the self is where we connect to the energy of our ancestors, and draw on their accumulated wisdom.

Too often, the destructive energy of racism contaminates our minds and disconnects us from our cultural essence. We become afraid and suspicious

We need to understand and embrace our political self.

This aspect of our self is where we learn how to handle the power that money and position offers to us, and decide whether to use that power – or lack of power - for positive ends or to abuse others.

Too often, the ruthless pursuit of self-interest and the arrogance of class or caste systems sets us at each other's throats and creates endless conflict.

We'll look at all these aspects of self in turn. Gaining awareness of each one is another important step on the journey.

Throughout history people of all cultures have created their own representations of god/dess, designed to look like themselves. This is how it should be, this is not in itself a problem.

The danger has been when people begin to force their own particular metaphor of what the god/dess looks like on others. Even worse, they then murder people for not agreeing to their particular representation of the creator.

This is the sort of abusive and dysfunctional behaviour that societies have manifested, and is all about power, control over others and is totally ego centric.

God/ess is a universal energy. It is the language of the heart.

It is the universal drum within the pulse of life, within the womb of the universal mother. It is the universal energy of the creator that flows through every single living organism and through it we are given the choice to manifest our being-ness.

Of course we are made in the image of god/dess.

Of course I am made in the image of god/dess. So are You, of course.

CHAPTER SIX

Your Natural Self

The society we live in at the moment is one in which we are at war with our natural selves.

We are at war with nature; we are at war with emotions; we are at war with anything that is different or we don't understand. We have to be in control of everything.

The biggest enemy of our modern western world seems to be the emotional sphere. The domain of the emotions, which are the language of the heart, and the intuition.

The contradiction in our western world is to my mind quite astounding: on the one hand it is professed that there is no room for sentiment or emotion; they are seen at best as weak and at worst primitive and unintelligent, getting in the way of sound judgement. Then, when society has worked so hard to detach men and women from their emotions, people cry out in outrage at these "monsters" who commit terrible crimes of murder and brutality against humanity. Faced with adults torturing, sexually abusing and murdering children, and teenagers torturing and murdering each other, with parents and children turning on each other, and men and women brutalising each other, the media frenzy reports:

"Brutal and senseless killing!"

"The evil monster showed no emotion!"

"S/he must have had psychopathic tendencies..."

Well I have news for you! These people are *not* monsters. They are products of a society which has played a part in conditioning them to become the way they are: emotionally disconnected, indifferent and cold, frozen even.

How can you teach people to live detached from their emotional centres and then expect them to show compassion?

People end up being psychopaths by many different routes, and it is not always in the genes as some would have you believe, but for the most part they are created by the society we live in. When you live in a society that shuns emotions as weak and unworthy, we either accept the negative label of being weak ("like a woman!"), or we begin to suppress and deny our own feelings.

Without emotions, unable to hear or speak the language of the heart, we become psychopaths.

Emotions are an essential part of the creative universe: they help us experience our life, they keep us present and in tune with each other and are one of the gateways to our spiritual experience.

Someone called Paul once pointed out to me a very interesting scene in Bruce Lee's film "Enter the Dragon", where Bruce Lee, while teaching a young student gives him a slap around his head and berates him, "Don't think! Feel!" Very interesting, because in the so-called "civilised" world boys, girls, men and women are slapped around the head literally and culturally, with the message: "Don't feel! Think!" Talk about out of balance!

This is the reason we can abuse and murder the earth

at the rate we are doing. The pulse beat of the earth is emotionally connected to all that lives on the earth. We are so far separated from our feelings that we can no longer hear her, nor can we hear each other. We can no longer read the signs nature is giving us, the signs that are trying to tell us that mother earth can no longer support us and nurture us the way she once did because of the abuse she is suffering.

She is being poisoned and torn apart. Her innards are being ripped out.

And by attacking the earth we are attacking our own natural selves.

Every living thing is made up of the same 92 atoms. They may be arranged differently, but the essence is the same. That essence is our natural self.

Our bodies are made of water, minerals, electrical energy, chemical energy – in fact all the same stuff that the earth, sun and stars are made from. Wow! We are infinity itself…

As we poison the earth we are slowly but surely poisoning our own selves.

Next time you go to your local supermarket, have a good look around. On display in front of you appears an abundance of nature's produce. Fresh meat and fish, pink and gleaming. Huge piles of shiny, juicy-looking apples, pears, bananas, oranges, from all round the world. Vegetables of all sorts – clean, bright and fresh-looking – in a dazzling variety of colours, shapes and sizes.

You would think we live in a paradise of abundance! We in the western world are told that we've never been so well fed and so healthy. We should be happy and grateful.

Funnily enough, many of us feel anything but happy! We eat more food, but somehow don't feel better for it. The food looks so good, but is somehow tasteless. Our fridges are full, but somehow we feel empty.

In the words of Bob Marley's song "Mi Belly Full but Mi Ungry Still".

If we look behind the carefully created illusion of the supermarket shelves, a very different reality emerges.

Animals that are being made to produce time and time again and are not allowed to nurture that which they have given birth to.

Baby animals separated from their mothers and made to live with the screams of the slaughterhouse always in their ears.

Fruit ripped from the mother tree before it is ripe and which has not yet finished suckling nutrients from its mother. Have you ever noticed how that lovely super-market fruit often looks ripe and sweet on the surface but when you bite into it tastes dry and at times is rotting on the inside? The outside is nice and shiny and waxy yet the fruit itself is rotting at the core which is the heart of the fruit. It is literally dying from the inside out.

If we're not careful we'll be like that fruit: looking good on the outside but feeling heartsick and finding life tasteless and unfulfilling.

It's time we looked after our natural selves, by looking after the natural world from which our natural self is made.

Are you aware, for example, that without the trees we would not be able to live? Without them breathing in the air first and transforming it from poison to something safe for us to breathe we would all be dead. The trees are our outer lungs; they breathe in harmony along side us. They are interconnected to us; they are not separate from us. We are co- dependent on them (yes, not all co-dependence is bad!) because they enable us to breathe. It is a symbiosis.

So the next time you decide you are going to chop that tree down because you are fed up with having to sweep the leaves off your designer path, don't think, feel! Ask yourself how you would feel if you were held responsible by your future family members for being part of the generation that murdered the trees, just because you didn't like the leaves on your path!

You should be honoured to sweep the leaves up and to give something back to mother nature. It's the least you can do - it's called reciprocity.

And if you don't like trees go seek help! Or go live in a desert someplace.

I hear enough of you quoting the saying, "what goes around comes around". Well, what about helping what comes around to be a blessing instead of a curse by help-ing to work with nature instead of trying to control nature?

Do you know that if you cut a tree it bleeds? – it's called sap. Do you know that trees have a language and if you spend time with the tree people they will talk to and nurture you? I know some of you will think this is all new age clap trap, but in fact the wisdom of the trees is a very ancient universal lore. Long before any "new age clap trap" your ancestors knew the significance of the trees. That's why in some parts of Africa the pla-centa of a new born baby is buried in the earth and a tree is then planted on top: universal connections to the rhythm of life (how beautiful is that?). So the next time a baby is born forget the bling and buying a gold chain; go plant a tree!.

Anyway, don't take my word for it, test it out for yourself. The next time you are feeling sad or upset take yourself out into nature and just allow yourself to be in her company. You will feel her in your heart. If you go amongst them, the trees will talk to you if you let them, but the language they speak is the language of the heart - that means to be able to commune with mother earth, nature and trees you have to be able to feel.

The trees are just one aspect of nature; depending on your own particular inner self, you may feel connected to flowers, animals, insects, birds, fish or even rocks! It doesn't matter, as long as you are empowering your natural self to grow and work in harmony with nature.

Our planet Mother Earth is in pain and is crying out for us to slow down, and to stop depleting her resources faster than she can give birth to and nurture new resources. There is a natural cycle to everything and each Mother has her own cycle that is in tune with the universal rhythm of its own life cycle.

Nature speaks to the heart and the heart is the gateway to spiritual dimensions of being. Our ancestors knew that, just as the Native Americans knew it. When Chief Seattle tried to warn what would happen if the white man continued to abuse mother earth, his words sadly fell on deaf ears, because those who seek to conquer and control were (and still are!) blinded by their own ego centric superiority, arrogance, lack of feeling and greed.

Now, the prophecy of the ancients is coming to pass. Our Mother Earth is in danger and in pain. We are in danger of being threatened with the same fate as the

Atlanteans, Lemurians, the ancient Egyptians and many others before us if we don't get our act together.

Each one of us has the power to do something about this, yes, especially you!

I'm not asking you to stop shopping at supermarkets, or to turn vegetarian, or to eat only organic food, or to "go Green" or any other colour! If you want to do any of these things, that's OK, it's your choice and if you are guided by your divine self it will be the right choice.

I'm asking you to make a change inside your self, not simply a token for a week or two.

Begin to relate to Mother Nature as you would a treasured friend or loved one.

Talk to her. Respect her feelings. Be kind and considerate. Apologise to her if you make a mistake, she is all forgiving.

Don't take things from her without asking permission, and always say thank you. Think about what you can give her in return.

Through doing these simple things, you will give your natural self the power to change the course of history, to change the course of destiny.

You will re-connect your natural self with the heart energy, the language of the soul.

Naturally, it will be you. You, Co-Creator.

CHAPTER SEVEN

Your Sexual Self

Relationships are so important on our spiritual journey. They can help us move forwards, or they can hold us right back.

And sexual relationships are especially important, because our sexual energy is closely connected to our spiritual energy.

Men and women can do great damage to their spiritual and emotional selves by misusing sexual energy. In fact it is the poor state of relationships between men and women in modern societies that is one of the biggest problems for people trying to understand their inner selves. Male domination, misogyny and the attack on the sacred feminine have led to a situation where sexual relationships can too easily tip out of balance and right now they are sooo sick and dysfunctional they are in need of intensive care.

If you're ready, I'm going to spend some time exploring the ways in which our sexual self can become disconnected from our divine self. Sexual energy is so powerful because it is the divine energy of creation itself. And because it is so powerful, its misuse and abuse can have very powerful destructive effects on our inner self.

We mess around with it at our peril.

Let's look at the example of what happens when a man or woman has been sexually and emotionally betrayed by the person s/he thinks s/he is in a loving relationship with. After the initial shock has worn off we often feel an intense period of anger which then gives way to a deep-seated sense of betrayal. At this point all manner of insecurities find their way from the soup of our emotional energy centre. Past issues resurface. Such issues as rejection, abandonment, not being good enough, can overwhelm us.

Seldom is our first thought: "why is this person so inadequate or dysfunctional that they are not able to form relationships without having to have either an escape route, play games or betray and deceive you with another person?" Because remember - nothing just happens! The person had to have the intent in the first place...

"It just happened!" they say. I don't think so! Everything has a starting point and this is no exception.

First the person has to have made a conscious decision to have a conversation with another person. At that stage a decision is made internally whether they like or fancy the person, or what ever the intent and motivation is - we don't know what energy response is operating inside another person. Remember that there is a process to everything, including sleeping with - no let's tell it like it is - staying the night with someone in order to have sex with them, one night stand or not.

The verbal diarrhoea of "it just happened!" belongs in the "yes, but!" category, and the "I don't have to take responsibility for my actions" camp and a pretty pathetic place that is (meeooow!). If you are going to do it at least own it. It gets even more pathetic and dishonest when it comes to the next time it happens! "I cant help it!" It's what men/women do!" Oh really…

Because believe me, with the "it wasn't my fault! It just happened!" brigade, there will without a doubt be another time, no matter how sorry they present themselves as. If they won't own it they don't have to take responsibility for it. It just happened to them! Ok the first time may be a mistake but anything after that it is an intention.

This is usually the kind of relationship in which all the rejection issues the person has are played out. Sometimes if we have not at least acknowledged to ourselves that we have certain fears then we will forever either test the person we are with or choose dead end relationships with men or women who are so screwed up that they will never be able to form a deep and meaningful relationship.

People need to wake up and realise that the energy from the previous person you have slept with will be carried by you into your next encounter with the person you are supposed to be with. The energy from that person will – whether you want it to or not – flow in to the other relationship.

This can be a deep and frightening experience. In fact, this is one form of psychic attack. It is usually unintentional but sometimes deliberate, some people set out with the intention of trying to destroy another person's relationship.

At this point let's pause and see if you're ready to continue. This can be a difficult part of your journey, because of the powerful part your sexual relations (or the absence of sexual relations) play in your life.

Pause for a few moments and reflect on any sexual relationships you are in at the moment. How do you feel about them?

What about relationships you may have had in the past? How fulfilling were they? What life choices did they reflect? What were the reasons that caused the relationship to end? Are there any similarities between your current relationship and your past ones?

Are you looking for a new relationship? Are you seeking a new sexual partner? What are you hoping to gain from this? Is it a positive choice, or is having someone better than no-one? Are you afraid to be on your own?

Or have you decided that it is not the right time for you to be in a sexual relationship? Is this a decision based on a reaction to a painful experience? Is it to do with your feelings about your health, your age, your attractiveness to others? Or maybe you have decided you need time to heal?

Are you prepared to look deeply into your past, present and future sexual relationships, from the perspective of your divine inner self?

To what extent do you feel your sexual relationships have helped you to connect to your inner self? To what extent might they have caused you to disconnect and disassociate from yourself?

The answers may come clearer as you read on.

But remember, this is not about blaming ourselves or others for mistakes, or beating ourselves for poor choices. This is about learning from our experiences so that we can make better choices in the future.

At this point let's not get confused between having sex with someone and making love to someone - there is a whole world of difference, believe me! When you have truly made love with someone the energy is very special and you never forget it.

Whichever it is – having sex or making love - not only are you in the person's personal energy space, but you and the other person's auras are intertwined and already at an energy level exchanges are taking place; exchanges of all the five senses and, at other-dimensional energy levels, exchanges of thought forms. Whatever is going through your head when you are creating sexual energy is important – what are you summoning up? Or calling into being?

Casual sex? I thought so too, but you know what? Forget it – there's no such thing, especially for women! It's a dangerous, and completely unbalanced way of thinking about sex.

Equally as unbalanced is the idea of "recreational sex".

There are always entities hanging around which will find opportunities to connect to streams of energy consciousness. For women, because men penetrate us and enter inside us, this can happen unwittingly.

Be aware, you cannot wash energy off unless you do it consciously by intentionally and ritually cleansing the energy field.

Those men who have several female sexual partners at the same time are mixing different energies together, a kind of energy alchemy. Some may do this out of sheer lack of responsibility or to appear macho. Others know what they are doing and deliberately place another woman's energy inside of you. Once that's happened, that's where the two energies will do battle, from the inside. Oh yes, it's deep!

Some couples choose to have multiple partners but

this must be by mutual consent, and many of these relationships do not seem to last. Unless the different people involved have given permission to have their energy taken and mixed with others', the energies will be incompatible, or compete with each other, or may even poison each other.

Sounds far fetched? Well consider this. You know when we women are around other women - say friends or family members - our periods synchronise and we all harmoniously begin our sacred bleeding time together.

Well HELLO the energy of the woman your man has just placed inside of you synchronises your period to her energy! So your periods will change to synchronise with hers, thus beginning the power battle on all levels, the most obvious being the emotional.

The energy battle about to take place its not just a physical act - that means nothing. It is ALL levels: emotional, psychic and spiritual. It affects mind, body and spirit and can be a huge trigger for a spiritual emergency. Every thing affects everything else.

So, sisters, you know when you get that feeling about him and you just know he is seeing someone and he denies it and you say "I know it's true, I just feel it", well of course you do! You are feeling her energy. Remember the old saying, "I feel it in my water"? How wise those elders were who said that!

And by the way, my brothers, the man is walking around with the energy of the two women clinging to him and incidentally he is not, as he may have been led to believe, in control!

This is because neither of the women's energies is in harmony with his. Because he has created the disease (DIS-EASE) in his own energy field this can lead to all manner of karmic reprisals, including physical illness, and sometimes even spiritual emergency or a temporary emotional breakdown.

Carrying a conflicting energy in to the psychic field of another person who trusts you and introducing negative energy thought forms in to their energy and thought field, is creating a war. You can't expect to start such a conflict and get away with it. For those of you who understand computers, it's like introducing a Trojan and not expecting it to have an effect!

I am not going to be upset if you disagree and think this is clap-trap. Don't take my word for it - examine your life and see for your self if any of this fits. Don't just think about ex-partners, speak to them; ask them!

Many of you men will find out that your intimate partners knew at an intuitive level that you were having an affair with a particular person or were about to, or had slept with them.

Maybe you lied about it, trying to fool them into thinking it was all in their head. A lot of people do.

Don't be such an egotistical fool! They never believed it. You didn't fool them at all. No, they went along with it and pretended to themselves that they believed you, because they thought they loved you. How tragic is that? You were fooling no one, but hurting every one; your partner knew at an energy level that you were unfaithful.

Worst of all, you were not just messing around with another person. You were messing with the energy field and the creative energy of dimensional interconnectedness. This interconnected dimensional energy field is the energy that is created in sexual union with another person.

Both energy fields combined together to create a trinity of energy; it's the same as when two people are chanting or singing and a third vibrational sound starts to resonate that takes your note to another height and it feels as if a third musical note or another vibrational sound has been created and joined to your singing or chanting.

It's the third energy presence that enters every living thing and forms the trinity.

It is effortless and in tune and feels quite awesome - you actually feel it resonate inside you. Musicians quite often experience this other energy presence when they are in a place of total harmony with other musicians. It's that place of musical precision or cosmic unity where they and the music are one. Awesome – that's a spiritual encounter.

It's the same with sexual energy. It's emotional and spiritual alchemy, a third frequency that attaches itself to yours when the right conditions are created. This energy is not something you create; it is already in existence, just as electricity is or radio waves or the pulse of energy that exists in a quartz crystal that is placed within watches to balance time or used for healing. Marvin Gaye sang about this energy in his song Sexual Healing.

It is the birthing energy of the universe.

I'm going to say that again.

It is the birthing energy of the universe.

Sexual energy transforms itself and creates a third vortex of energy. It's a kind of alchemy that takes place and is the gateway not just for the creation of the soul of a child to enter, but opens the way to negative thought forms and entities.

It's all down to YOU. What is manifested through sexual energy depends on where you are resonating from at that moment in time.

Whatever is born from your intentions at that time is carried in to the energy field of you and whichever other person is engaged with you at that particular frequency.

Let me give you a typical example of this. Take the situation where a person is being unfaithful to their sexual partner. Imagine that the long term partner does not know on a conscious level about the affair, but on an intuitive energy level their inner self knows.

Say there is a resentment towards the long term partner from the woman he is having the affair with. In this situation the unfaithful partner comes home steeped in the other woman's energy and is then intimate with his long term partner. By the way, this does not have to be the same day or night the energy is with him as long as he is in the relationship with the other woman - and often long afterwards – depending on the intensity of the encounter.

It doesn't matter whether the man has had a shower or not, because you can't wash energy off that easily. That's why when women are raped they still feel dirty even after scrubbing themselves over and over again; it's because they can still feel the energy of their attacker around them.

Through his sexual activity he has introduced the vibrational energy pattern of the woman he has been unfaithful with in to his long term partner. All the negative resentful energy the other woman feels for his partner is energetically carried right into the heart of his relationship.

It's like placing a foreign body or injecting a virus right into the heart of the relationship.

And if his relationship with the other woman has been going on for some time, even more damage is done because of the battle that takes place at a psycho-spiritual level. Many wise people describe this as a psychic attack and quite often with this form of psychic attack the long term partner's periods may change to synchronise themselves with the period of the other woman.

If the vibrational frequency is compatible, make no mistake, a gateway is created for the birth of this energy entity to attach itself to your energy field. You then become host to this entity. This entity could be carrying all sorts of energies – anger, jealousy, fear, resentment – and these will become active in your psyche and in your relationship with your partner.

Sounds far fetched? Well I'm not here, remember, to tell you what to think! But please, have a think about some of your own experiences, and see if the idea of sex as an exchange of psychic energy begins to make sense of some of the experiences you have had, or you have seen other people go through?

To talk of energies may appear at first sight to be a strange and off key way of looking at what on the surface can be seen as people doing their own thing and having a bit of fun.

But wait. There are times when within sexual relationships a climax can be reached that goes beyond and is much more intense than the feeling of physical gratification that one gets through orgasm. It is possible to experience such an intense emotional charge with someone that it flips you right into another form of experiencing, it's as if you have flipped right in to a different dimension.

Have you ever experienced this? If you have it will be because you connected to someone on a deeper level than the merely physical. It can be a truly metaphysical experience.

In Indian culture an aspect of this is known as the

Kundalini energy, an energy that lies dormant within us, nestled inside like a coiled up snake. This energy rises up through the spine and energy centres within our bodies – known as the chakras - and into the consciousness of a person's being.

During sexual union it can be so powerful that the experience can literally alter your state of being for a short period of time, rendering you unable to move. It's at that moment that you can feel like you are floating. Some people have been known to have an out of body experience at this time, while others have experienced a pleasant falling or drifting feeling as if they were falling in to the other person, sometimes through the eyes (the eyes are after all known as the windows to the soul).

The sexual chemistry that is created between two people in a relationship can be so intense that they can usually sense each other's energy approaching long before they see the person with their physical eyes. They feel them in their energy system.

That's why it's important to know about the depth of sexual energy, and have all your senses and wits about you while making love with someone. For it's at these times we are at our most vulnerable and open to energy flowing into and between us from other dimensions.

We are at our most creative during a sexual relationship and we open a gateway not only for the soul of a baby to enter, but the energy and thought forms of entities that are in the atmosphere with either positive or negative intentions.

Why should this be thought strange? After all most people would agree that music is vibration and those vibrations affect us deeply. The beat of the drum is akin to our very own heart beat; the rhythm of the music, the tone of the voice, the sound and tempo of the saxophone, all create strong feelings inside us - it is not called soul music for no reason.

In that sense, sex is no different from music, and at least as powerful. Put them both together, and…Why do some people persist in seeing it just as some form of one-dimensional physical pleasure? It is far, far more than that.

Think about your last relationship break up or that of a friend. The chances are you or your friend played lots of sad songs about loss – we are using music here to externalise how we are feeling. Sex is used in the same way, whether we want to really admit this or not. One night stands, aggressive or abusive sexual practises, are ways to devalue relationships. It can be a way of proving to the world "I don't need anybody!" or it can be used as a weapon to devalue the other person.

Making love can be a truly spiritual experience and can create a third harmonising energy that can tap into all kinds of incredible experiences.

It can also be used to tap in to all kinds of sick and demonic thought forms and energy dimensions.

It all depends on the intent; it's the intent that calls the energy in to being; it's the intent that determines the outcome of the union. So you see you are responsible for what you co-create.

The Sacred Feminine and Sacred Love

During my research into people's experiences of counselling I recall one woman in particular, who talked about the Kundalini experience and related how she tried to discuss this with her counsellor. She found although he was nice enough and was trying she was sensing he was not getting it and the counsellor, eventually admitted he was afraid of what she was talking about.

It made me wonder: why it was that Men are so fearful of a woman describing an intense experience like this? It shows how out of balance our culture is when men become afraid of female energy.

It also reminds us how much effort male-dominated religions have made to crush and destroy what they feared so much - the sacred feminine.

By making God a man - *he* this, *he* that, *his* love, *his* - and putting everything male and masculine on a pedestal above female and feminine, modern religion has completely ruined the balance of male and female energy needed to keep ourselves and the universe healthy. Christianity, Judaism and Islam have a shameful history of trying to confine women to second class status. Not only have they pushed women into being little more than producers of babies, they have also tried to claim that the only purpose of sex is procreation! What complete rubbish this is.

What we have to remember is that religions of this kind are man made and were created by men. I don't have a problem with this in itself and I believe that these religions have a right to exist. What I do have a problem with however is that man made religion wants to dictate to me and take away my choices as to what to believe. It's a form of bullying to tell others that their spiritual practices are heathen and demonic - how dare they!

What I do see as evil, demonic and barbaric is the amount of historical blood Christianity, for example, has on its hands. Now that *is* barbaric. Not all people came to Christianity through love and freewill; many were forced into it historically through fear and torture, which included the rape of both male and females. Along with rape and torture were murder and looting – all, incredibly, in the name of God! What a projection! Yet when an individual murders and tries to impose their will on another and then says they are doing God's we'll lock them up as criminally insane!

If anyone thinks I am making this up or being unreasonable I don't blame you - it seems to have been airbrushed from a lot of history books. But please, just do your own research into the history of Christianity; dig deep, it's all there.

If you wanted to you could find out about the many sacred goddess sites from ancient times that some of the churches are built on. I don't know about you but if someone tells me that a particular plot of land has evil energy I'm not going to build my house there, would you? No! But the church did, right on top of the sacred Goddess sites.

Male dominated religion has taken and destroyed the feminine symbols and goddesses and transformed them into masculine versions. Worse still, religious organisations have demonised the feminine, as in the story of Eve leading Adam astray - as if Adam was not up for it - literally! (Sorry, just me being naughty…)

This shows that the early Christian church was well aware of the power of these sites. They knew a great deal about sacred female energy wisdom. They couldn't destroy it, so they set out to control it.

This in turn created a space in which misogyny – the outright hatred and rejection of everything female and feminine – took root in societies dominated by masculine religions. Which led to thousands upon thousands of women being tortured, drowned, burned alive and beaten to death as witches mostly healers, herbalists, wise women, midwives and the politically minded.

Misogyny, and the abusive behaviour towards women – and towards men who display "weak" feminine tendencies - has a terrible history, and is behind a lot of the abusive sexual practices that have wreaked havoc with people's emotional and psychic wellbeing.

More of that later, but for now let me say once again, I'm not against religion or churches, I just object to people creating churches that seem designed to exclude people or attack those who don't share their perspectives. Who said religion has nothing to do with politics? The decision to oppress women and remove almost all trace of them from the spiritual and religious domain was a political one, as was demonising women's sacred bleeding and labelling it a curse.

Too often we allow these churches – often as much political organisations as religious ones - to claim to possess the only way to connect with god, through men that represent the son of god.

Well I'm sorry - it is women that actually give birth to men! Men do not give birth to themselves - a scientific fact. It takes the combined energies of masculine and feminine to co-create a life. But women give birth to this new life, to themselves, and they also give birth to men.

Does not all life start as female? All humanity has its beginning in the female. All life has to pass through the female before it can develop into a life form. Again, don't take my word for it: you can check out the scientific evidence for this if you want to. That's why the word male is singular and the word fe-male contains within its essence masculine and feminine. The same with the word woman, which contains the energy of both male and female.

The female is energy, is spiritual consciousness, a sacred space where all must pass through the gateway into being from the divine.

Now it's important to be clear that all of us, whether born physically male or female, are made up of both masculine and feminine at an energy level.

All of us contain a balance of male and female energies. In fact, achieving a good balance between the masculine and feminine aspects within ourselves is an essential step in our journey.

And this has nothing to do with what has come to be called our "sexual orientation". Our sexual preferences – whether we choose sexual partners of the same sex or the opposite sex – are, like everything else, a matter of choice.

Each choice we make, because it expresses our inner intent, creates energy vibrations, so it does make a big difference in all sorts of ways whether we have gay or straight sexual relationships. The task of creating a balance of sexual energies in our lives and within ourselves is the same, although we face very different challenges depending on our sexuality.

Masculine is not better than feminine. Nor is feminine better than masculine. They are two complementary expressions of the same divine energy.

When they come together in harmonious creativity, through a healthy sexual relationship, we can connect directly to our divine selves.

In the right circumstances, with the right partner, we can discover this for ourselves.

Now this is where you can do something very practical through which you can experience tremendous healing and empowerment.

But first of all you need the right partner. It may be that this is not the right time in your life, or that the nature of your relationships don't make this desirable or possible.

If this is not the right time for you, it's because you are going to experience the incredible energy of the divine in a different, non-sexual way, perhaps through your natural self, or your cultural self.

But if this is the right time, don't hesitate! Practice sacred love making and experience it for yourself. Make love with the right intention be conscious and stimulant free and be present and in the moment; connect to the energy.

Sometimes people can feel a little scared if they are not used to making love in a tuned-in way, because they start to experience things they have not experienced before, feelings from the heart and not just the groin.

This is because they are only used to having sex with the five senses and not with the whole of their being. The experience, because it is so powerful and so different from base sex, can be quite daunting at first to those new to it.

However there are a number of things that can be done to prepare for this experience.

The first is to choose to be fully conscious of what you are doing, without the influence of alcohol or drugs. Including Pot, draw, herb, hash, or what ever else you choose to call it.

Take some time to prepare yourself mentally, emotionally and spiritually.

Choose a quiet time and cleanse your self and your environment with incense and oils.

I quite often use either a sage smudge stick to cleanse the environment or frankincense will do just as well.

I also make for myself a cleansing and relaxing bath. It is also good some times to give your aura or energy field a bit of a cleanse either by smudging or by preparing an aura spray with herbs and essences and oils of your choice. If you don't have any of these you can add sea salt, which is also an energy cleanser, to your bath water. This preparation is good because it removes all residue of other people's energy from you and it turns your intention and energy connection inward to the universal, sacred and creative love juices of liquid energy.

There are teas you can make to heighten your senses or you may just choose to relax yourself. If it is your first time practicing sacred love making, you can do this by making some chamomile tea. It is used to calm and relax you so can just as easily be used to relax you before your sacred encounter.

Above all, ask for the divine energy of the creative essence of the universe to be with you for the highest good.

This is the true meaning of sexual union. At the moment of climax there is a point of stillness, true stillness, which has been said to be the closest man comes to god.

I prefer to use the word god/dess because it contains the essence of both masculine and feminine energy. God/dess contains within it the combined energy of man and woman (womb/man), female and male, masculine and feminine.

The sacred energy of all the universe: uni (harmony at one) verse (song poem). Uni~verse: in union with the song of creation, the song of life.

Making love is dancing to the rhythm and pulse beat of the universal energy, the pulse beat of life.

The dawn chorus of the song of life... the birds offer to call in the blessings of a new day.

This place of stillness is the point where sacred female and male energies come together. The female energy lies inside the womb. The male energy enters. So when it is said that man is closest to God at the time of climax, we mean that man is closest to the womb.

Closest to the sacred mystery of creation. The Goddess (ence) within.

The sacredness we carry in our self.

CHAPTER EIGHT

Your Cultural Self

It's time now for you to pause again in this journey.

Time to reflect once more on your self.

At some point, many years ago, a man and a woman brought their sexual energies together to create you.

Yes, your mother and father.

Interestingly enough, we use the word "conceived" to describe the moment when male and female energy combine to create a new life.

A conception is both a birth and a thought. So the creation literally thought you into existence.

Think about your mother. What sort of a person is she (or if she has passed on, was she)?

What do you know about her life at the time she conceived you, carried you in her womb, gave birth to you? How old was she?

What energies do you think were around her at the time you were conceived, and with what intent were you brought into being?

Think about your father. What sort of person is (was) he? How old was he?

What was happening around him and within him at the time he conceived you? What was the energy of his intent, when, as the saying goes, you were "just a twinkle in his eye"?

If one or both of your parents are alive, you may be able to ask them about this directly. Depending on the people they are, and on your relationship with them, you may or may not get true answers, or any answers at all! They may not be ready to share that part of their life with you so you need to respect that choice.

These are important questions, I hope you agree. The answers could tell you a lot about yourself, and the journey you are on.

What aspects of your mother's energy do you think are part of you? Do you look like her in any way? Talk like her, move like her, behave like her, and think like her?

What aspects of your father's energy do you recognise in yourself?

In many families, especially when young children are around, there are often conversations between family members about these things.

"Doesn't he look like his dad?" "She's got a temper like her grandma!" "Where's she got that red hair from – is it from her mum's side of the family?"

Don't worry if you didn't know one or both of your parents physically, if for example you were adopted or grew up with only one parent. There are still clues to be found by looking within your own life – things unique to you that can't be explained by your early childhood experiences.

If you want to know what your parents look like just look honestly at yourself in a mirror. I mean truly look in the mirror, not from a place of ego or vanity. Go past concerns about whether you look good, past your hairstyle and glasses and earrings, past the superficial and into who you really are. You will see your mother and father looking back at you. Their energy is in you and will metamorphose itself on your face.

Look deeply into your own eyes and you will see your parents looking back at you.

At this point ask yourself the question: who am I? The answer may surprise you...

In many traditional cultures a child is named according to the energies that are around him or her at the time of their conception or birth. The naming ceremony acknowledges the importance of the invisible energies and potential present at the birth of each new child.

In traditional cultures there has always been a clear understanding of how sexual energy links families together, to create a tribe, a group of people linked through shared genes. This forms not only a village or community, but through shared experiences and shared practices, what we have come to call a culture.

You can see how this works at a cellular and energy level if you consider how a baby is formed in the womb.

The child is made up directly of the mother's blood, so carries all the mother's cells, and cells, we now know, carry memories (DNA). Modern science has rediscovered what traditional cultures have always known intuitively and instinctively, the power of genes to influence humans across time.

But at a deeper level these genes carry not just memories but the spiritual, emotional, intellectual and psychic potential of the mother and her bloodline, going back ancestrally, as well as all our future untapped potential to surpass the limitations of the previous generations.

In the double helix of the DNA spiral this female energy is joined in a dance of life with male energy.

Through the genes we are linked at an energy level to the past and the future.

Stepping into this reality has been described by some cultures as stepping in to the "dream time", or by others as "entering the realm of the ancestors", and by others as connecting with the "collective unconscious".

Once we get this at the true depth of its meaning we can pool our inner being with the generations that live inside us and whose power and energy we can call up to empower, guide and nurture us.

Closely entwined with our sexual being, therefore, is a powerful cultural being.

This cultural being embodies the accumulated experience and wisdom of the ancestors, family, and community into which we are born the collective consciousness of which we are part.

Our culture is around us and inside us.

What we all need to do is to develop our cultural awareness and our skills of cross-cultural communication.

This, you might think, should be an easy and enjoyable experience, because we all can take pride in our cultural background, can't we? Surely we all have so much to share, and our own cultural being can only be enriched by joining in a dance of celebration with other cultural beings?

Unfortunately we have all been contaminated by the poison of racism.

The distorted and destructive energy that lies at the heart of racism has driven cultures apart, and led to cultural genocide, to holocaust.

Demonic energies have been manifested through institutions such as slavery, Nazism, Apartheid, and the celebration of cultural difference has been transformed into a living nightmare of cultural destruction.

This has affected everyone on this earth. You, me, us.

If you therefore continue on your journey with me you must be prepared to look at racism, and the potential for racism that lurks in the way we validate or dismiss areas of experience that are a vital part of spiritual exploration, such as initiation, rites of passage and healing ritual.

Your potential racism.

It amazes me how keen most people are to remain in a state of ignorance and confusion about matters of race. People of all backgrounds can start talking nonsense because of our wish to avoid looking at the reality of what racism has done to twist and distort our spiritual selves.

For example, how come you still hear people saying "I don't see your colour"? Of course you do! It's one of the first things we notice about one another when we meet, before we even open our mouths. Personally I love my colour and want you to see it as an integral part of who I am. If a crime had been committed and you had spotted me at the scene and someone asked you for a description I bet you'd soon recall my colour!

The issue is not if you see skin colour or not, but what your response is to the colour you are seeing. What is taking place inside you when you see someone of a different colour?

Is saying you don't see my colour meant to be an attempt to communicate to me that you are seeing me as an equal? If it is, please see my colour as part of me and still embrace me as your equal.

Part of our spiritual journey is to see human diversity in all her expressions, of which colour and culture is a vital part.

This is not the time to go into a lengthy description of the awful history of racial and cultural abuse. If you haven't already educated yourself about this, next time you go into a book shop, you can choose one of the many books that will help you understand better. If at all possible, find a book that will tell the story from the perspective of those on the receiving end.

It's worth taking some time, because so much of the ancient wisdom of the ancestors has been buried under the tsunami of racism. For those interested in a spiritual journey, so much of the spiritual knowledge available to us from different cultures has been pushed to one side by racist thinking. Or worse still its origin has been airbrushed from existence, or presented as new age.

I use the word traditional to describe people's way of life because I am fed up with the constant use of the word "primitive", which I find offensive. It implies that ancient or tribal peoples are in some way backward or of poor intelligence. (And no, I'm not being "politically correct"; I'm being culturally respectful.)

The fact is that some ancient peoples were able to achieve things we are unable to achieve today, even with the technology we have; for example the precise mathematical calculations and perfect alignment of the pyramids, in Egypt - their precise mathematical precision existed long before Pythagoras - or what of the huge Nasca drawings in Peru which can only be seen from the air , or the huge sculpted Olmec heads on Easter Island, to mention just a few.

I think we are very arrogant to describe other people's way of life and traditional practices, both past and present, as primitive. So I hope you have noticed how I refuse to refer to any persons or traditions in such a manner as to label them in a way which implies they are somehow below the level of another.

Over and above the effect that racism has had in belittling, demeaning or dismissing the wisdom of other cultures, its most damaging effect has been to introduce fear, anger and hatred into the depths of our cultural selves.

We really need to heal the wounds that have been inflicted on our cultural selves. But this has proved to be more difficult than you'd think.

The problem is it means looking at some very unpleasant realities about what people possessed by negative thought forms about others can do to each other.

For example, how many people have really bothered to find out what was actually done to people, say, during the incarceration of millions of human beings during slavery? Such a polite word to describe the incarceration and attempted genocide of a people. As soon as this subject is mentioned many people close down and start saying, "here we go again! Why do they always go on about something that's in the past?"

If only those people could show the same open mindedness they would to war veterans when each year they wear poppies and talk about the horrors these men experienced and witnessed in their wars, even though it is now a long time in the past they always say we must never forget, quite rightly but we too must be granted the same honour. We too must be allowed to remember and never forget.

If someone in your family was murdered or tortured, would you expect people to say to you, "well that was in the past, stop talking about it now!" That would be like saying to people affected by tragedy that their families' lives meant nothing and that they don't have a right to remember them.

We all have a right and a duty to remember those who have suffered, because through that remembrance we can learn some really important lessons we need to learn on our spiritual journey

I understand you might be more than a little shocked at some of the acts perpetrated during the dreadful psychopathic act labelled slavery. An example of this would be the attempts of a young girl - and I mean girl (paedophilia was rife among the slave masters) trying to escape the daily torture of being repeatedly raped and beaten whilst pregnant by her substance abusing (alcohol, and opium) and at times syphilis riddled master. (Again, check the historical records).

When she was caught, not only was she further subjected to rape and a severe beating she was made to stand bloodied and naked in the middle of a circle of other pregnant women and girls who were forced to watch in case they too got any ideas of trying to run away from the atrocities they faced. She was then subjected to a further beating before finally being murdered by having her unborn baby cut out of her and thrown to the ground where upon it was left to die as a warning to the rest.

Others who tried to escape were stripped naked and tied to horses who themselves were beaten and forced to run in different directions thus literally tearing the people apart. This sadistically evil behaviour was carefully planned; it had to be first thought through. It was created in the psyche, in the energy centre of the internal system long before it was manifest and birthed in to the physical world.

On a much deeper level - on a psycho-spiritual and energy level - it was also used deliberately to transfer the stress, trauma and fear from the mothers forced to watch into the unborn foetuses they carried. The mothers' fear and anguish is transferred through their chakra energy centres down the umbilical cord, where it fed directly into the psyche of the child through to the sacred water sac and saturated directly into the developing energy field of the child. The sacred sac the child is laying in becomes steeped in a vibrationally charged concoction of fear and trauma at a cellular level and this is transmitted directly into the DNA of the child.

In this way a disturbance has been created in the psychic centres of the child, and this creates a post traumatic stress disorder which travels down the generations into the present.

Many writers have now recognised that whole communities in America, Europe and the Caribbean, are still suffering the after-effects of the slavery experience. It has been called "Post Traumatic Slavery Syndrome"

It means that people living now, who have no direct experience of slavery, still feel its effects on their psyche and soul at an energy level.

Who knows? Maybe my ancestors were slaves, and yours were involved in the slave trade. At an energy level our relationship is still carrying the echoes of this trauma, so despite all our efforts to relate positively, we may still find ourselves uneasy in each other's company and at times find it difficult to connect.

To make things worse, there is a lot of bottled up, blocked up stress and trauma within the community due to the denial of the abuse that took place during this period in history and the atrocities that were committed.

Why is it okay to acknowledge (quite rightly) the Jewish Holocaust, the atrocities committed by other Africans upon their own people, such as Idi Amin in Uganda and the Massacre in Rwanda (again, quite rightly), but not the psychopathic act of slavery? Why is that? Have you ever wondered?

I can't help noticing that when the English or Americans are involved in atrocities they are played down and quickly covered over, or worse still just simply airbrushed out of history altogether .Yet the English and American media is forever commenting on what the Germans did during the war. If it was the Germans, not the British and Americans, who had played a huge part in the psychopathic act of slavery, would it have also been referred to as such an atrocity - one that must never again be repeated?

The word holocaust means "burnt offering", "wholesale sacrifice or destruction" according to the Oxford dictionary. Yes, I can see why they would have chosen such a description to describe the experience of the Jews in Europe under the Nazis. I wonder what description would be unique to the African experience? What one word could capture the essence of the sheer volume of what was done?

At least if there was a word to describe the experience, African and Caribbean communities could begin to talk

about the real meaning of it. At least if it was acknowledged and talked about in the media, if there were statues
and parades and speeches commemorating its survivors,
then those whose ancestors were possessed as slaves
could begin to heal.

And if we can begin to talk about it – yes, you and me
– then we can begin to heal the wounds our cultural selves
are carrying.

Let's pause again, and check some things out. Find a
quiet place once again, and a few minutes in which you
can reflect on your cultural self.

What do you know about the culture of your ancestors, on both your mother's and father's side?

Were any of your ancestors involved in traumatic
events, such as war, slavery, colonialism, which brought
them into conflict with people from other cultural traditions?

Are there any echoes of these conflicts in your present
life?

What contact do you have with people from other
cultural traditions? Do you have direct experience of
them as people, or do you rely on what you have been
told about them? How fearful or suspicious are you of the
cultural other?

Do you feel particularly comfortable or uncomfortable around people of particular cultures? Be as honest as
you can within yourself.

If you have a significant relationship with someone
from a different cultural tradition, particularly if you are
in a sexual relationship, it is very important that you
spend some time finding out as much as you can about
the history of their ancestors and yours. At a subconscious level there maybe superior and inferior roles being

acted out in your relationship not intentionally but through conditioning.

If there has been a time when your ancestors and theirs may have come into conflict, it is time to take steps to heal the ancient wounds.

The simplest way is to acknowledge consciously the hurt that has taken place, and to ask for forgiveness from your divine self.

Do not for one moment underestimate the effect of this simple but very powerful acknowledgment.

Working with your Cultural Self

It's important for all of us to develop a positive sense of our cultural self.

High cultural self-esteem is an integral aspect of a healthy self.

For many of us, there is ready access to positive and uplifting images and rituals relating to our culture.

If you are from a European Christian culture, there are magnificent churches and cathedrals, if you are a Muslim, increasing numbers of beautiful mosques.

There are books and paintings and music that all project a positive, confident image of English, American, French, Spanish, culture, for example.

The problem here, as we have found, is that quite often the psychopathic savage side of the history of these cultures is airbrushed out of the books and pictures. You have to search to find the truth, in order to be able to clear and cleanse your cultural self.

It's a quite different problem if you want to gain a positive relationship with one of the cultures that has been on the receiving end of racism and colonial domination.

Many traditions outside Europe, from Africa to the Native Americans to the Indian sub-continent to the islands of the Pacific, have been systematically suppressed.

Take the example of a person of shared heritage born and brought up in England who has a direct line to their African genetic bloodline through either their African mother or father. If this person has never seen African symbolism or only seen the Hollywood fictional version of the meaning of those symbols they will start off with a negative perception of the meaning of African symbolism right from the start.

The particular problem here is that it is almost impossible to process positively inner visions that are connected to images whose meaning and interpretation has been dominated by racist Hollywood movie style visualisations. In these fantasies, Africans and other people of colour become the cultural "other" who are to be demonised and feared as deviant, different and dangerous.

Incidentally in the sixteenth century a debate took place within the Catholic Church as to whether black folk (African people) had souls or not! If they didn't have souls, it was argued; they should be treated and classified the same as animals. After some time it was decided that they did have souls after all - how very gracious of them. This gives you some indication of how the cultural other has been viewed!

I feel a question coming on here... can I just ask: who decided if white folk had souls!?

No wonder then that the mixed race person in my example might appear crazy, mixed up and self hating towards the African aspect of self.

Interestingly enough in my therapeutic work I have come across people whose parents have both been black and they too have had issues with their own black identity. Such is the power of racism.

All aspects of African symbolism have been labelled as "voodoo", and "black magic" – characterised as dark and devilish.

What one has to remember is that all this is happening at a subconscious level of being where we internalise all images we see, without exception. Symbols are the language of the subconscious.

Symbols and pictures are the direct language to the gateway of self, and more importantly the solar gate to the ancestral realm and the multi-dimensional realm of being.

The symbolic realm leads us into the very depths of our psychological, emotional and spiritual being.

Because those of us of African Caribbean heritage are always being shown reflections of ourselves associated with negative, demonic and satanic imagery, this representation of us has now been connected to and woven into the very fabric of our music.

Gangsta rap? A mixture of pornography, misogyny and violence? Where the hell did that come from? And more importantly who in the music industry is promoting and encouraging such expressions of psychological, emotional and spiritual genocide?

As I have said, music is vibrational and the vibrations resonating at a particular frequency co-create and birth into the world an entity in the form of energy that attaches itself to a compatible intent.

Just listen to the music that young people in our communities are now listening to and creating, and the video images that accompany it.

This is a psychic attack at a very, very deep level. A form of internalised genocide. A direct hit on the psychological and spiritual centre of our being.

We really need to stop being so shallow and regurgitating all this rubbish about being individuals and doing what we want because it's our life and nobody can tell us what to do. It is your duty to protect yourself from psychic attack and connect to your higher self.

Okay, I can just hear some of the young people now: "Who the f**k does this b**ch think she is? Telling me how to live my life! I'm an individual..." Can I just ask can you tell me what other men of different cultures do you hear sing about aiding the emotional and spiritual genocicide of their own woman? Do you really know the power of what you are doing? We are not individuals; we are connected psychically.

You are connected to the divine essence. Your cultural self image is part of that essence. You do what you think, you manifest what you sing.

Lose that connection, and you have left yourself open to invasion and control by negative, destructive energies, what many of us call "fourth dimensional entities".

Our true self-image is the key to our perceptions, not just of others, but more importantly of the essence of self and who we believe our self to be.

It allows us to enter into the symbolic realm without being accompanied by the negative imagery of those who would do us harm.

The symbolic realm, which is the very core of our existence and the fabric of our being.

Let me tell you about a period many years ago during which I experienced at first hand the power of ancestral energy. I entered the dream time with little understanding or preparation.

I experienced vivid images of a woman with three heads and a dog with three heads attacking me, chasing me. The dogs were lunging at me while the three women's heads looked on, one watching me, one mocking me and the other trying to speak to me.

I was terrified. I had seen this image on and off for years I was about eleven the first time I saw it.

I didn't want to go to bed on my own. I was literally scared to go to sleep on my own in case I died; that's how terrified I was. By the time I was a teenager I was afraid to say anything either, because some people already thought I was weird so telling them would have really put the icing on the cake and confirm me as a candidate for the funny farm!

The woman who used to come to me in my dreams and terrify me at that time I now understand to be Hecate. She is the wise woman in Greek tradition standing at the cross roads who represents change and she can appear very scary.

The collective consciousness is filled with all manner of images. We are not just flesh and blood, we are multi-sensitive and multi-dimensional beings.

At an even younger age another recurring image of a huge back to front bird used to appear to me in my room along with strange people. I used to call them the statue people because they were always there. My parents always told me not to be so stupid they were just bad dreams. But these images terrified me. Why? Because as a child I had seen all the black and white films about "savages" who would attack people for no good reason and then twist their necks around along with that of a chicken for no good reason other than they were black. (Oh, sorry, "savages" was a word used to describe non-Europeans all the time then.) And one of my school reading books as a child was Naughty Little Sambo - I kid you not!

So as you can imagine when this bird with its head facing backwards appeared to me along with non white faces, I as a child, recalled all the images that had been placed in my memory bank, which came flooding back, and with no spiritual and emotional enablers around to act as guide, my experience was dismissed as that of yet another crazy mixed up half caste kid. (As a teenager I once peeked at my doctor's records in the days when they gave them to you to hand to the doctor and there in bold letters were the words "West Indian Social Problems"! Anyway, back to what I was saying…)

What was really happening was that I was tuning in to the dimensions of African ancestral consciousness. Unfortunately I didn't have the knowledge or the courage to know how to get help from wise Africans who were surely around me at that time. There were too many ignorant attitudes around about mixed race people being "not African enough".

At that time I was in a spiritual desert and terrified. Unknown to anyone I was going through an awakening, with Visions and Images all connections to my genetic cultural bloodline.

I now know that the image of a back to front bird was the Sankofa bird from Ghana, where my father is from. Years later it would be my understanding of this experience that would lead me to reclaim my name on my birth certificate which is ANKRAH - my father's name. (My mother had changed my name as a child by deed poll to my stepfather's name when I was seven years old.)

The vision of the bird with the twisted round head and the statue people I now understand symbolically to be my father and grandmothers psychically and telepathically connecting with me and not wanting me to forget them. Sankofa is a symbol which is about going forward but not forgetting your past; that's why it walks forward but looks back.

As for the scary woman with three heads, this was connected to the idea of a crossroads - change, choices and transformation, and came from my mother's European cultural tradition.

So actually archetypes from both my cultural and spiritual heritage were coming through, not in a conflicting way, but in a harmonious way. It was only terrifying because I could not read the symbols. In fact they were complementary of one another, an example of my inner cultural yin and yang working in harmony.

What a shame I had to go through such an ordeal to find this out! But at that time, because of the effects of racism – the ignorance and fear that had been created around non-European cultural wisdom – I had no way of receiving the images positively.

My cultural self was starved and undernourished. The wisdom of most of the peoples of the world was being denied to me.

This, in the end, is the real harm that racism wreaks: negative relationships between cultures keep all or part of our cultural selves closed down and dysfunctional.

Oppression of aspects of the other – other cultures, other traditions, other beliefs – is in fact oppression of an aspect of our self.

So how are you going to work with your cultural self?

The first thing is to embrace all aspects of your cultural self.

The next thing is to work towards releasing yourself from the miseducation of racism, and for that you need an open heart and mind.

This is not an easy process, nor a quick one. And I can't help you directly, because only you can know the full story of the different traditions – positive and negative – that make up your own cultural self.

But perhaps my experience will help. It's the experience of a woman who was born of an African father and an Irish mother, in a place and time where neither cultural tradition was acknowledged.

It's the experience of a woman of shared heritage who was born in a time and place of overt racism. Signs saying "No Blacks, No Irish, No Dogs" were common to see when people were looking for a place to live.

Here, then, is my affirmation of my cultural self

A Declaration to People of Shared Heritage

It is time for people of shared heritage to stop warring with aspects of ourselves and the world - it's a waste of our divine right before god and the ancestors to be here.

We also need to stop apologising for existing! If people don't like it they will have to find a way to forgive themselves and get over it. Our divinity is here, we are here and we also have wisdom, knowledge, intelligence and things to teach others about their own humanity.

Just like all others you are children of the universe and have a spiritual destiny and purpose to fulfil, just like the rest of the guests on this planet we call mother earth.

Let's put a stop once and for all to any self hating and loathing and having to choose one aspect of our being over another. People with an African or Caribbean parent or grandparent should give up trying to prove they are "Black enough" to others and focus on becoming whole enough for yourself, or trying to prove you are white enough to fit in we are who we are.

People known as "mixed race" have to struggle through all the negative energies that swirl around in a racist society just as much as anyone else.

You need to work at embracing all aspects of your divine being in order to function as the multi-dimensional being you were created to be.

It's time shared heritage people stopped allowing themselves to be the scapegoat for past transgressions. The creator did not make any mistakes with you!

It's time to grant forgiveness to yourself for the things your ancestors may have done. You are not to blame.

The goddess has blessed you with a divine right to be here, so embrace your divinity and allow yourself to shine, give your gifts to the world.

Your ancestors will guide you, if you have faith. Do you really think your ancestors are out there in distant stars and inside you in your genetic memory agreeing with all this claptrap about you? Do you really believe your ancestors are that mean minded? They and you are part of the universal fabric of the web of life.

You don't need anybody's permission to call yourself African! Your mother or father gave you that when they gave you your African blood that flows through your very veins.

You have a direct line to your cultural, spiritual, ancestral lineage if you so choose it and I strongly suggest you find out all you can because someone may be trying to get through.

And remember: nobody has the right to define who you are. Your mother or father saw fit to give you life, so who are others to judge against the divine blood that flows through your veins?

Embrace your ancestors and they will embrace you. You are they and they are you. They live inside of you, just as a sapling lives inside a tree. You can get on with the business of connecting with aspects of your spiritual self that are working in harmony.

If I am at war with myself as a person of shared heritage then my life archetypes will be at war with each other, because that's what I will tap in to, call up and summon into being. But there can be peace in the inner landscape.

I now call upon the energies of all the different aspects of myself as a person with both African and Irish genes inside of myself and in my psyche. I have the right to call up, tap in to and be guided by my African ancestors who live inside of me regardless of who thinks I am black enough or African enough. Those are judgements that belong to others. The truth of who you are runs through your veins.

My African father along with my Irish mother, with the blessing of the creator, saw fit to give me life and there is no higher authority than that of the creator seeing fit to birth me into this world with my shared heritage.

Coming from a shared heritage of Irish and African I will call on any deities I wish to assist me, be they African or Celtic.

And I pray that others will embrace the different cultural dimensions of their spiritual selves as well.

For this does not only apply to those like me who are an African, and Irish mix; this applies to all people of shared heritage, be it African, Caribbean, Spanish, Indian, Chinese, English.

Let the images and archetypes flow from all the streams of our lineage.

Let us remember as we journey the Sankofa symbol of Ghana.

We can walk forward into our future but also look back and remember where we have been and bring with us the wisdom and the best of who we are and what we have learned for the highest good. The wisdom of our cultural self.

"I Am Whole

I Am A Woman, I Am A Man.

I am a Child, I am a Teenager.

The Ancestral Heritage of my Mother and Father Flow through me, I am a being of shared heritage,

Born into the world, the fact that I am here on Mother Earth gives me the Divine right to embrace myself and the heritage that flows through my veins.

I am a child of the Universe, the Song of creation.

I have a right to be here, I am an Expression of the God-dess

I Am Whole, I Am Loved, I am Blessed."

CHAPTER NINE

Your Political Self

How are you feeling at this point in our journey?

Are you feeling a sense of growing awareness about the issues and challenges in your life? Have you begun to see other people differently, to recognise the energy patterns that are flowing around your friends and family?

Are you feeling, perhaps, a little better about yourself? Less inclined to beat yourself for being inadequate or for making mistakes; more inclined to forgive yourself and look forward to the birth of your better selves?

I hope so.

Or are you feeling a bit depressed? Perhaps feeling horrified and disgusted at some of the examples I have brought up of just how cruel and vicious people can be to each other?

Are you feeling weighed down by the sickness of misogyny and racism?

I hope not.

Our souls are not sick. A soul is a beautiful thing, part of divine creation.

What can happen, though, is that our emotions become damaged and our ability to connect with divine energy is weakened, at times even lost.

This is caused by various forms of abuse. Abuse allows negative energy to contaminate our energy system in just the same way as our immune system can be weakened and broken down.

In order to heal our selves at this deep level it is important to be aware of the various forms abuse can take.

Not in order to get depressed, or to get lost in sad and distressing reflections. That would weaken our soul's "immune system"!

No, we need to be aware so that we can strengthen the positive energy of our inner selves and radiate light where there is darkness, raise up that which has been cast down.

This is where politics and spirituality are inextricably intertwined. The contradictions and dichotomisation of a society based on institutions set up by men addicted to power can cause confusion in our minds.

This is why we need to embrace our political selves. Politics, at an energy level, is not about the ridiculous puppet show of Prime Ministers and Presidents and parties and policies.

It's about what lies behind these games: behind the uses and abuses of power.

Not power used to control others but the power used with the intention of empowering our self and others.

The abuse of power, or power used to abuse, in its most extreme form, is power used to possess and destroy other human beings.

This is all about seeking to control other people's psyches, in the mistaken belief that it will increase one's own power. It may increase your power over other people, but that is just temporary and will soon disappear. It certainly won't increase the health, happiness or wellbeing of your soul – just the opposite in fact.

It's important therefore to develop your political self in order to strengthen your defences against various forms of aggressive power play.

In many cultural traditions this is known as the "path of the warrior", or as "martial arts". These are not practices that are simply about physical fighting; they are about psychic self-defence. They involve body, mind and spirit in taking care of oneself at a political level.

Remember the "Victim Leeches" I introduced you to earlier? Well people who seek to gain power over others through various forms of bullying, intimidation and abuse are another, more dangerous type of energy thief.

They are called Energy Vampires, and they are a lot more active in their way of stealing your energy. They tend to reel you in as part of a deliberate attempt to take something from you. They range from your conman to your abusive control freak, to your psychopath.

What they have in common is that they plan to take you over and even to possess you at an energy level.

The energy leech is quite often not aware of their toxic effect on people because they are so caught up in their own pain and are so sorry for themselves they cannot see their own toxic behaviour as any thing but justified. This is not intentional but dysfunctional.

The power hungry energy vampire on the other hand has a plan for you. What you are dealing with here is someone who is showing you that they have the potential for abuse, and this could be the sign of someone who possesses a dangerous, malevolent energy. They are clever and calculating.

As with all bullies, energy vampires will quite often start by abusing the weak and helpless, such as young children.

When children are sexually abused it has an adverse effect not just emotionally and physically, but at the level of the soul and spirit.

If a child or a woman has been repeatedly abused energy patterns build up around them. These energy forms connect and vibrate to a particular frequency, a bit like when a person who is afraid of dogs gives off a smell and a dog can pick it up. So too can predators, whose intent it is to target a child or woman, sense that fear and trauma.

Different forms of fear give off different smells and energy. Different entities and thought forms hang around the energy field of the child. You can sometimes see it very clearly. A term that is often used to describe abused and neglected children is that they have "a haunted look" and this is precisely what happens at the level of the soul. Their energy field is haunted by the cluster of entities who feed off the possibility of a perverted sexual encounter – sexual vampires in short.

Such encounters have nothing at all to do with sex but everything to do with power, control and possession. It is about the total control and crushing of a life form.

This goes beyond your opportunist child abuser or your emotionally screwed up rapist who has many hang-ups about women, usually stemming from hang-ups with his mother.

This is someone who is consciously seeking power. And is usually in cahoots with others using abuse for financial gain.

So if you sense that someone you are with is a sexual

energy vampire wait for the first opportunity to get away from them and don't hesitate to take it. And if you can, try and avoid any further contact with them. If you have to see them – perhaps they are a family member, or someone you have to work with, or the friend of a friend – keep your defences up at all times. And if possible try not to be alone with them.

Most importantly, tell someone, find your voice; that is the one thing that frightens them. Exposure

And don't be fooled by appearances! Sexual energy vampires, or abusers of power, are not as portrayed in so many books and films, brutal looking working class men, or dark-skinned foreigners.

These behaviours are also carried out by men who are outwardly respectable, well off, well educated, and well dressed. Well spoken men who are often in the business of making money or hold positions of trust, power and leadership. These men are often protected at an organisational level by their position. Predators and paedophiles come from all walks of life.

It's important to understand that these atrocities can be carried out by all people from all social standings. Sexual criminality and the negative energy attachment associated with it, is not the domain of certain classes or cultures. Persons of "high breeding", as they used to be known, well bred gentlemen of good manners, have been repeatedly guilty of atrocities to wo/man kind, yet their barbaric and evil behaviour has gone mostly unchallenged by many, and still is to this day.

In fact, those that are supposedly "above our station" are huge perpetrators of abuse, and violators of the laws they supposedly uphold, both morally and spiritually.

The fact is that those who gain wealth and power in

society are often in the best position to get away with systematic corruption and abuse. You have only to look at the numbers of priests who are now being revealed as systematic child abusers, often known to and protected by the church. Or the recent uncovering of those police officers who have been caught with images of child pornography on their computers. Because they have the influence to bribe others to look away, they have come to believe they are above any law, human or divine.

Abuse is classless, colourless, accent-less, financial status-less and educational-less: it applies equally to those from Oxbridge or from state schools, to lawyers, professors and doctors, as well as those with no formal education. The rape that takes place in the institution of a prison by male inmates and officers is the same rape and abuse that takes place in the public boarding schools of the upper middle classes - the only difference is social and financial. Rape is rape no matter how posh the accent or how huge the bank balance or what the position on the job description reads.

If you have any doubt, just listen to those brave souls who have had the courage to speak out and have too often been silenced by accusations that They are liars or mentally unstable, loose cannons or just plain criminals whose stories are fantasies.

The effort made to silence those who would dare to speak out is not surprising; after all those perpetrators have reputations and positions of power to protect so they will attempt to silence their victims by any means necessary. But who reports the personal abuses and corrupt behaviours of those responsible? What about those who, far from exposing the crimes of the powerful, see it as their job to protect them from any exposure? In the words of the old saying, who is judging the judge and who is policing the police? Look at the recent allegations made about the police officer who perverted the course of justice in exchange for money from a known drugs dealer, the father of one of the murderers in the Stephen Lawrence case.

In order to develop your political self it's important to look at social class and status, and the overt and covert uses of aggression.

And for those of you who I have heard profess there is no class system because supposedly we can all eat and are not living in the depths of poverty, I suggest you think again!

The very warp and weft of the society we live in, in Britain is based on class and bloodline.

Wealth and power is still a very strong feature in our society and some people have a lot more than others. Within certain families – tribes might be a better word – wealth and power are handed down through marriage and birth. In other words through the sexual energy systems we looked at earlier.

Just because some of us may have "good" jobs and have moved up the economic ladder a little does not mean that the class system has suddenly vanished. As soon as you live in this society you are in and become part of a class structured system - it is part of the fabric of this culture; if we live here we become part of it and are affected by it.

How aware are people of this? Well, it depends on who you talk to. It's certainly not a topic that gets much coverage in our so-called "free" press!

When I was a rape crisis worker I noticed that the crime of domestic violence and rape affected people from all backgrounds, yet rarely was this reflected in newspaper reports or TV programmes. The myth that middle class women do not experience rape or domestic violence was well and truly blown out of the water for me during my time at the rape crisis centre. I was working with middle class women both as colleagues and as victims.

The reason for the myth is the private hospitals many of these women could afford to attend. Their bruises and broken bones were treated in exclusive private wards away from the questions of social workers, police or press reporters. Often because the perpetrators were from these very professions.

It soon became clear that a lot of these women had no one to talk to and were therefore very alone and isolated, something that had never occurred to me before. At that time I, like so many others, was under the naive and somewhat ignorant impression that, because these women appeared to have money and spoke with a posh accent, well, what problems could they possibly have? It never occurred to me that their husbands might be controlling their finances or that they may be being beaten behind closed doors.

Not surprisingly, those who are most involved in the abuse of power are those who are most reluctant to talk about it, or even to acknowledge that there is such a thing as the class system.

Try a little experiment yourself. Ask friends around you and people at work which class they think they belong to. Ask them what they think about the class system. Do they think it exists? If they do, what effect do they think it has on them?

You may find that some people get quite uncomfortable talking about these things. In my experience it's the more middle class than upper class people that find it hard, or even those of us who could once shout working class slogans in the seventies and eighties but now find ourselves being able to live a middleclass life style. It is difficult to talk about class whether we are black or white because there is such a thing as a black middle class that has its own set of dynamics. I say this from my own personal experience of my own family life, growing up in a very working class family in Moss Side and contrasting that to the people who came into the area to work, whether black or white and to my husband's experience of growing up in a middle class black family in a suburban area of Birmingham.

Whatever social class you were born in to, and the social position you now find yourself in, may well influence the responses of those around you.

It has certainly influenced the development of your own political self.

Being aware of the power that you have by virtue of your position and wealth is very important.

More important is choosing how to use that power to fulfil your spiritual purpose. This means turning away from the abuse of power, and avoiding getting drawn in to any of the "power over" games people play.

It doesn't mean avoiding positions of responsibility, and leadership roles. Just be sure that you don't abuse your position, but use your authority to pursue higher goals.

With power and the abuse of power all around us, we can't simply sit on the fence and pretend we're not part of it. Our spiritual journey involves making choices day in day out.

Personal Power and Responsibility

Have you ever been around someone who has said, "Ooh! You missed it last night - it all kicked off!" They then go on to describe an argument or a fight they witnessed.

Well, I have news for you, Have you ever considered that the person already picked up that something was about to happen on an energy level before it happened, they knew it was about to kick off; they picked it up long before the first punch was thrown or angry word was spoken!

The energy (or "atmosphere") in a place changes long before an angry word is exchanged or a nasty look is communicated. You can pick it up in the air as thought forms gather just like animals do before a storm.

You know the (old crone) wisdom sayings: "I can feel it in my bones"; "I feel it in my blood". Of course you do. Your blood communicates to you. It is a living thing; it knows the language of the unspoken.

Have you ever been around some one who literally made your blood crawl and you didn't know why, but you later learned something very worrying about that person's behaviour, and you said to yourself, "I knew it!" Of course you did.

So consider this: why did this person now telling you about this incident stay to watch a violent attack on some-one? What did they do to help? Because standing and watching is not helping, it is another way of being involved.

Sometimes by staying and watching the risk of harm or injury is minimised. This is called watching with consciousness from the heart. Your presence as witness may bring a stop to what is happening, as in the case of police brutality. If they know people are watching corrupt police officers are unlikely to go to the extent they went to in the horrific beating of Los Angeles citizen Rodney King. In these cases by staying you are indeed helping. By bearing witness.

But if you are staying to watch just to see what happens or who wins, or because you never liked the person being attacked anyway, you might as well be the one doing the attack.

You certainly are attacking at an energy level if your energy connects up to the energy of the person doing the attack and fuels it and feeds it and gives it life and sustenance. That is why sometimes when a person attacks someone and they don't stop it is because they are carrying out the will of the group at a psychic and energy level: the ferociousness of the attack is determined by the level of negative psychic energy injected into the situation by the crowd.

This is another form of vampirism. All those who are watching and doing nothing to help are feeding off the negative energy contained within the violence and aggression.

By being a bystander you have shared in the abuse that is taking place. Your decision to stay and watch was a political act.

Let's look honestly at the energy vampire within ourselves, not just the ones we see around us!

Mind Your Language

One last, important thing: mind your language.

Language and the way we use it to describe and

communicate who we are and who is the other, is very important.

In the beginning was the word and the word was and is very powerful. It has an alchemy all of its own which influences thoughts, feelings and behaviour. How we describe some one or something affects the way we see it, think about it, and in turn respond to it.

You don't think so? OK, try the following exercise:

Ask a friend to read the following to you.

"Close your eyes and imagine this. You are on your own, walking down a dark street and there is a gang of eight yobs hanging around. One of them has a stick in his hand and is waving it around menacingly. All the gang are drinking alcohol, shouting and behaving in a threatening manner."

Now answer these questions:

What images came into your mind?

How did you feel?

Now ask a friend to read this next piece out for you.

"You are on your own walking down a dark, badly lit street, very late at night and there are a group of young lads mucking about in the street, one of whom is a prankster larking about with a stick. They are all in high spirits, having a bit of a drink, talking very loudly and making a bit of a show of themselves."

What images came into your mind?

How did you feel?

What was different this time?

Did you feel as uncomfortable or as fearful as with the first description? I doubt it some how!

The first one painted a very negative and threatening picture, and this is often the language used in news reports and papers to describe the behaviour of young people from inner city working class families both black and white.

The descriptive language used to describe the same behaviour in young people from middle or upper class families paints a very different picture of the same behaviour.

Your back ground and social standing is paramount in determining how you will be referred to, what language will be used to paint a picture of you, and what sort of feelings will be conjured up about you.

A good example of this is the word "aggression". Oddly enough aggression is always the domain of the "other", never the self.

Aggression has been delegated to the cultural other, and the working and under classes. Aggression in the middle classes, especially the White middle class, is all but denied! When people speak about responding to aggressive behaviour and dealing with antisocial behaviour, this is usually about dealing with the Black and White working classes. And the new underclass is a constantly changing mixture of black, white, Asian and now Eastern European and East African populations.

Language, the words we use when we communicate with each other, the words we choose when we talk about each other and when we write books about each other, is another form of energy.

So please, be careful about the words you use.

When you use words like "primitive" and "uneducated" about native peoples, you are giving energy to those who wish to belittle their achievements. Education is culture specific. What's the point of being able to use a computer if you live a nomadic life style? Surely the education needed would be to learn which materials to use to construct the best weatherproof dwellings or what berries are edible and which will kill you. That is culture specific intelligence. Put you or I in that environment and let's see who is primitive and uneducated, shall we?

Chances are that without the educated intelligence of the nomadic people to guide and educate us our chances of survival would be slim.

When you use derogatory words to describe those who are poor and marginalised in our societies you are giving energy to those who want to keep power to themselves, by labelling others as not worthy.

When you use words like "bitch" and "booty" in your song lyrics about women, you are giving energy to those who want to attack the sacred feminine.

It's not about being "politically correct". It's about being true to your political self. Personal and cultural respect is to do with divine wisdom and universal balance.

Whoever wrote "sticks and stones may break my bones, but words will never hurt me" was talking rubbish! In the African tradition, a person is not dead when their body has been destroyed, but when people stop using their name because the energy of their name is lost.

When we give names to people, or to things, we charge them with a certain power or energy. The power of an intent, a thought-form.

That's why the art of using language effectively is such an important thing to learn. Unfortunately, not everyone gets access to this education in our society. While middle class children are taught the importance of asking questions as a sign of intelligence, and are encouraged to practice asking questions, working class children are taught to follow orders with out question and are not encouraged to ask or question. The message that is given from an early age is, "do not ask questions! You will show your ignorance and you will appear stupid... listen to others, they know best..." If working class children, or children from the inner city ask a question they run the risk of being called cheeky, or worse still disruptive.

In fact, asking questions is one of the most important steps we can take on our journey of discovery.

Remember, spiritual wisdom and knowledge from ancient traditions has been deliberately suppressed for many centuries. We are supposed to accept without question the version of reality that those in power have agreed is "safe" for us to know. Only by asking questions can we begin to challenge this system and regain our right to self knowledge.

That's why politics and spirituality are intertwined.

So just as the divine self is the questing self, so the political self is ultimately also the questioning self.

The aspect of you that asks anyone, including yourself, what does it mean to have power:

"For what purpose?"

"What is your intent?"

"How can I make a difference?"

This is not easy, especially in the face of power that is quite prepared to bully and intimidate.

Sometimes we have to be very clear about what is good for us and what is harmful, regardless of what people in "high" positions say.

Sometimes we have to stand against the crowd, and be prepared to be unpopular.

We have to be prepared to look at the truth, even

when it makes us and others uncomfortable. We also have to look at the ego and arrogance of those who feel that they alone have the sole right to decide who or what is "correct".

You do not have to wear the right clothes, belong to the right political group, be the right kind of African or European or priest or priestess or belong to the right religious group.

What you have to be is true, sincere and have the right intention in your heart.

The heart is not measured by how patriotic you are or if you are African enough or if you are from the right background or how many books you have read.

It is measured by the deeds you are doing and have done, and by the spirit in which you do them.

CHAPTER TEN

Your Shadow Self

So now you have gathered all your selves around you.

If you thought you were alone on your journey, you now know how wrong you were!

You have embraced your divine self, that inner core of your being that connects you to the god/dess and all of creation.

You have embraced your natural self, which is made of the same living material as the sun, the stars, the planets and the whole universe.

You have embraced your sexual self, which connects to the masculine and feminine energy of creativity, of the creation of new life, of birth and regeneration.

You have embraced your cultural self, which enters the dream time, and connects to the wisdom of the ancestors within us.

And you have embraced your political self, which uses wealth and position for the collective good, and connects power to divine purpose.

You are an amazing combination of soular aspects, possessing all the spiritual resources you need to heal your self and those around you.

But there is one aspect of your self to which you have not yet been properly introduced.

It's an aspect of our selves that lurks in dark corners, preferring to remain hidden from view. We have sensed its presence many times, as we have explored your many selves.

But we have not yet brought it out into the light, probably because it is the aspect of our selves about which we feel most uncomfortable.

Often we would prefer to remain blind to it, or if we catch a glimpse of it, to deny that we ever saw it. Even when confronted with it in plain view, many of us still refuse to acknowledge it as ours, preferring to imagine it belongs to someone else, to him, to her, to that other one over there - anyone else but us!

Yes, welcome to your shadow self.

This is the negative aspect of your self, the one that is quite capable of wishing harm to others, is quite prepared to bully and intimidate, is prone to thinking dark, wicked thoughts, and, in certain circumstances, acting on them.

This is the self that at times finds itself connecting to very negative thought forms, and when this happens it is like a kind of possession. The negative entity, energy or thought form attaches itself to our energy field and we then start to behave in ways that people perceive as "out of character". In actual fact it's not out of character, it's out of our shadow side.

But hang on, I hear you say, how can we have such a negative aspect inside us that is capable of doing such evil when you've said we're made of divine light? How can the god/dess energy within us become corrupted in this way?

Well, we're all born with potential; the potential that will be fulfilled in our journey through life (or, in most cases, through many lives).

We have both potential for light and potential for negative.

Think of us as a new born baby, having two energy sacs of potential attached at birth, one waiting to be filled with the potential for positive energy, the other with the potential to be filled with our shadow energy. Depending on the energy of those around our child –to begin with our parents or carers, later on our teachers, mentors and friends – these two energies can be fed and grow stronger.

If our child is surrounded by negative emotions – jealousy, resentment, anger, hatred, aggression, inappropriate lust, greed, and so on – then our negative energy is being constantly encouraged and nurtured. The positive energy is still there, but is weaker or can lie dormant, its potential unfulfilled.

As the saying goes, "the sins of the mother and father shall befall the child".

If our child is surrounded by the energy of love, wisdom, generosity and compassion, then positive energy is nourished and released into being. But don't be complacent; even then our negative energy still lies within us, like a sleeping beast. The fact is we have both.

We all have a shadow side, because that is the nature of the duality of who we are. Beauty and the Beast live within. From time to time all of us need to pause and acknowledge the negativity within us.

If you're feeling up to it, would you like to spend a few minutes reflecting on your shadow side?

This is nothing to do with blaming you, or punishing you, or trying to make you feel guilty. As I've said, we're all in this together. In the words of Jesus Christ, as he protected the prostitute from the men whose secret lust had manifested her into being in the first place and who then wanted to stone her to death for existing, "Let him who is without sin cast the first stone!"

This is about recognising something in order to deal with it effectively. As they say, the first step on the road to recovery for someone with a drink problem is to admit to themselves they are an alcoholic, or at least have a problem.

So spend a few moments thinking about times when you have been mean and spiteful, or dishonest and deceitful, and deliberately mean to someone else as an adult. What did you do?

How do you feel about your behaviour as you look back on it? Have your feelings about yourself changed since that time? What did you tell yourself about that person in order to justify your behaviour?

Do you feel you have made up for what you did? Have you apologised, either to yourself or to the people you affected by your actions?

One very powerful activity you can try is to ask your friends and families about your shadow self. Ask them "Is there anything about me that you really don't like? Or anything you find difficult and challenging?"

They may be reluctant at first, fearing your reaction to their words, but if you are asking with a genuine spirit they will give you the answers you need, not the ones you want to hear but the one you need to hear.

What you hear will certainly not be pleasant or easy listening for you. If they are being honest with you. It may make you feel vulnerable, hurt or defensive. The important thing is that you hear what needs to be heard in order for you to have a bigger picture of aspects of yourself.

But the idea is not to do anything immediately; just hearing about and acknowledging these aspects of your self is enough to begin a healing process.

Simply thank the person you have asked. Tell them how much you appreciate their honesty.

Afterwards, in the quiet and privacy of your own company, apologise – if possible, aloud - to yourself and to all around you. Be specific: for example say "I'm sorry that I sometimes shout at people to scare them into doing what I want." Or, "I'm sorry I'm sometimes so reluctant to share things with people." Or, "I am sorry that I verbally attack people when I am afraid." Or what ever it is you do.

Think about it: as you reflect on your shadow side, as you talk about it to your self and with trusted others, you are bringing it out into the light of who you are!

It's only that angry, hurt, frightened, resentful child.

It's already healing as you read these words.

But let's just explore the shadow self a little bit more before we move on. In particular, let's have a deeper look at what feeds it.

As you have reflected on your own experiences, it could be that certain patterns have emerged.

Are there times when your shadow side seems to come out more strongly? Does it happen when you are around certain people? Do these people remind you of anyone who has been in your life previously?

One thing is very important to know: the use of alcohol and drugs of various kinds can easily feed the energy of our shadow self.

This is especially true if we are already emotionally hurting and vulnerable. If we are not careful "a few drinks" when we are unhappy or upset can become a binge and before we know it we have altered our state of equilibrium which then disturbs our inner energy system and changes the frequency we are vibrating at. Our angry, hurt, dysfunctional self emerges from our shadow.

What happens when we indulge in certain substances without responsibility or purpose is that we can easily tap into the collective shadow, in which lies all the accumulated negativity of the ages – it is a powerful and dangerous swamp of negative energy. In it all manner of negative energy breeds and dark entities are waiting for the opportunity to harness themselves to a human host.

This kind of entity can usually only get through if someone is disturbed in some way. An example of this would be a teenager who is so emotionally disturbed that their energy vibrates at the right frequency for a poltergeist to attach itself to them.

But look what's happening right before our eyes, with young men and women going out week after week for no other purpose than to get drunk! This seems to have become a recreational pastime or sport which just as many girls and women partake in as do boys and men.

We live in a society where getting bladdered and kicking the shit out of another human being is considered by many – regardless of age - to be "a good night out".

We've also now reached the stage where sex is considered by many people as no more than another form of recreational activity, alongside a drink and a curry. Sex is now seen as something we do for physical gratification or to obtain a buzz. There is in fact little difference in people's minds between having a good punch-up and having a good shag - and incidentally the act of rape is fair game with this mind set.

In fact, people who use sex in this way are suffering

from a similar form of energy dysfunction as those people who use alcohol or drugs without responsibility.

This type of sex, known as "base chakra sex" is typically characterised by some form of abusive behaviour - either violent sex, or sex across the forbidden zone, including the rape of babies and toddlers and the use of animals - namely bestiality - and often involves the use of drugs and alcohol.

Common forms of base chakra activity include "swingers", sex orgies, prostitution, and pornography.

These are the sorts of base chakra activities characterised by a lack of any emotional engagement, usually indulged in by people who are out of their heads, or detached from their hearts due to abuse and trauma.

"Drink fuelled," you may say.

No it's not! Actually it must already be there inside, because the drink does not cause it or create it. Alcohol only acts as a release for what is already there inside of you; if it was not there already it would not be able to be released.

What's actually happening is our shadow side is being fuelled.

People who drink can be merry, sleepy, amorous, or jealous and violent; the drink inside them cannot create what is not there.

Drink is not the problem. People are. There is a place for drink but not if we are out of control as a people, and therefore cannot control the "demon" that drink can release

Sex, as we've seen, can release the sacred energies of creation. But not if it is out of the shadow side reduced to an animal activity performed by people whose feelings have been numbed by alcohol, and whose minds have been befuddled by drugs.

People are drinking, smoking dope and throwing all manner of drugs into their systems, altering their perceptions and calling into existence all manner of negative thought forms without a clue as to what they are calling into being.

Believe me, the things that are attaching themselves to people's auras without their knowledge are really frightening. They are what are known as "fourth dimensional entities", fourth dimensional because they exist in different dimensions of time – or nightmare time – outside time and space.

They are able to manifest because people are taking powerful mind-altering substances in such excess and with so little wisdom. Some of what is being taken should only really be taken for spiritual journeys or for an insight into other dimensions under sacred circumstances, with guidance.

But this society seems to have turned its back on spiritual wisdom. It has turned its back on Mother Nature and begun to destroy the balance of the natural world. Now that the earth is so polluted and the ozone layer is so damaged we are even more open to psychic attack than before. And the people who could help have been shoved aside in the mad rush to suck out more and more of the planet's resources while giving nothing back.

No wonder fourth dimensional entities are attaching themselves so eagerly to people, leaving their higher selves torn and shredded. With people who have had some form of negative attachment around them for some time you can actually begin to smell the negativity encased around them and even begin to feel out of balance when this person is around.

Have you ever smelled, or felt, or sensed an unhealthy energy around someone who is near you? "I just couldn't take to him /her?" we say. "There's something about him/her that gives me the creeps!" Well your intuition is telling you something – be very careful around this person, whoever they are.

Their negative energy is very likely to express itself through abusive behaviour towards you, or by inviting you to join them in some sort of abusive behaviour directed against others, usually verbal to start with. They never seem to have a good word to say about anyone.

These are the kinds of negative thought forms that can build up in the energy field of those who are dabbling excessively in alcohol or drugs; their energy resonates with the energy of the living addicted host, and attaches itself to them to feed off it.

Just as people can channel healing energies so too can people channel negative, sick or shadow energies.

These thought forms, as you can imagine, don't want the host to get well. Without attaching to a host these thought forms couldn't exist; they would simply shrink and wither away, just as a plant would if you were not feeding it. If they can be detached from the person they will eventually simply fade away and the person will gradually begin to reclaim their energy back and start to feel like "themselves" again.

Unfortunately people who are host to these forms of negative energy thought forms find themselves quite often very lethargic, low in energy, unmotivated, unable to see the point in contributing anything themselves but want everything without giving anything they are very bitter and blaming of others and with no desire to do anything to change their situation.

Others try to compensate for the energy that is being drained from them by trying to steal other people's energy.

They become, in fact, vampires, leeches, or perpetrators.

In other cultures, such as traditional African, Native American and many other cultures around the Globe, there was an understanding of the energy connections, and of the use of substances as a gateway to that connection. In ancient times people would use alcohol, chewing roots and smoking herbs, drinking teas and rubbing in creams with a purpose, to try and understand the nature of the creator within and the shadow within.

As a spiritual connection to the creator and the ancestors these substances were and have been used for thousands of years in a respectful way with people who could guide the person through their journey. Not like today, where these things are not used as part of a shamanic journey but purely to "get a buzz" and to get "out of one's head" quite literally to the point of unconsciousness. Or to deaden feelings, so people are literally like the living dead.

And today new substances have been created with no spiritual purpose at all, designed purely and simply to hook people.

You cannot control a substance like crack cocaine, its job is to control you. It's not up for negotiation; that is the intent of the people who created it. It was designed to kill you, emotionally, spiritually, intellectually, morally and eventually physically.

You won't find who you are in a bottle, or a needle, or

in a line of coke, or in an E tablet, or in a joint, or in bed with someone you hardly know.

You will find your dysfunctional self, or your shadow self. Or both.

And your shadow self will grow stronger, leaving your healthy self weak and shrivelled, increasingly unable to influence self-destructive behaviours and heading inevitably into addiction and death on all levels, the last being physically.

As with all things, it's your choice.

Do you choose life?

Which means having the courage to deal with whatever pain or issue you have and allowing yourself to feel.

To live is to feel.

To feel is to experience life.

To feel is to care.

You have to care about you.

You are worth caring about.

I don't know you, but I care. I care because you are a child of the universe, a son or daughter of the Goddess. We don't have to know someone to care.

Do you choose death?

By avoiding feelings and avoiding dealing with your pain you are choosing death.

If you don't know what I am talking about ask yourself this:

Have you shut down emotionally?

Are you able to feel?

Have you stopped caring about yourself?

Do you numb yourself with alcohol or drugs?

When you have a drink do you always end up becoming depressed and talking about all the bad things that have happened to you in your life?

Do you become destructive or aggressive when you have had a drink?

Are you bitter about your life?

If you can't feel, you are not living; you are existing.

If you can't feel, you are dead.

It's time to start caring. Embrace your feelings, start living.

Time to choose life.

CHAPTER ELEVEN

Spiritual Emergency

So where are you now on your journey?

If you're still reading this book, you must still be determined to take the steps you need to take to reach your goals.

Perhaps, through coming to know your many different selves, you now have a different sense of the challenges you face; perhaps you have different goals.

Whatever the case, as I said right at the beginning, this journey is one in which our spiritual self should emerge – a spiritual emergence which should be as natural as a flower blooming or a chick hatching from an egg.

But I hope you now realise that we live in a society where this natural emergence is not widely recognised or supported. In this society, too often anything to do with soul or spirit is belittled, mocked or just denied, and those who acknowledge a spiritual aspect to their lives are quite often ridiculed as weird, strange or deluded.

With alcohol abuse and indulgence in casual sex now promoted by multi-billion pound industries, this society seems more intent on calling forth our shadow selves than nurturing our divine selves!

In this environment, your journey might have become a struggle. You might well have experienced – or be experiencing now - a crisis, or what has come to be known as a *spiritual emergency*.

But what exactly is a spiritual emergency? How does it happen? Who does it happen to?

Let me begin answering these questions by sharing with you how I came across the idea of spiritual emergency as part of my own journey to understand myself and the people around me.

Throughout my life I have had a deep interest in the relationship between people, their emotional experiences and the search for spiritual meaning. What fascinated me was all the different ways people experienced their lives. Why did some people cope with life's pressures by drinking and others not? Why did some turn to drugs, while some to religion?

One particular feature of the community which I grew up in was the presence of a rich diversity of different cultures and backgrounds. Although it wasn't often talked about openly, there were people who had different ways of thinking about, and dealing with the physical and non-physical aspects of well being and illness.

A condition that might be thought by some to be best treated by physical means, whether through medicines or surgery, was by others considered to be best treated through prayer or other spiritual interventions, healing for example.

The "miracles" considered by some to be events that happened only in the far-off world of the Bible or the Koran, were discussed (privately) by others in ways that suggested that seeing visions, "talking in tongues", or being possessed by spirits were everyday occurrences in our own contemporary reality.

As I mentioned earlier on, I myself went through a period where I experienced great depths and extremes of emotions and feelings of intense affinity with nature, especially trees. Occasionally I would hear a voice that seemed to speak inside my head, and have internal dialogues with this other presence (which I now know as the voice of my intuition).

I have already described the way in which, when I tried to speak to people close to me about my experiences, they rapidly fell silent and withdrew, which made me begin to lose confidence in myself. What had begun as an extraordinary experience began to develop into a "crisis" in which I felt more and more uncomfortable.

At that time counselling was not an option for me (I had never even heard of it) and people around me began to distance themselves from me. Comments such as "pull your self together" were often spoken at me. I soon learned that people were afraid of what I was experiencing, and consequently became afraid of me.

If this is something you have experienced, welcome to a very large group of fellow travellers! I hope you can now begin to make better sense of your own experiences which may have been very confusing – even frightening – at the time.

I came through this period with new interest in psychology and spirituality. At about this time, through a series of conferences I attended in Manchester England, I was introduced (or guided) to the work of a group of scholars who were exploring traditional African psychological healing systems. I would mention here the books of Na'im Akbar, Wade Nobles, and Amos Wilson, all of whom point out that within the African tradition there is an emphasis on the interconnectedness of physical, mental and spiritual aspects of people's being-ness, which includes nature, trees, animals, etc.

I also began to explore beyond the confines of academic psychology, and started reading work by people who were interested in the connections between physical well being, emotional health and spirituality.

Another great book which was really helpful for me was "Interiors - A Black Woman's Healing in Progress", by Iyanla Vanzant. In this, Iyanla describes her own experiences of hearing the voices of her own intuition and at one stage in her life having these experiences labelled as "pathological".

Malidoma Patrice Some, in his book "The Healing Wisdom of Africa", describes in detail the healing traditions of the Dagara people of Burkina Faso where he was born and grew up, which teach about the interconnectedness of our individual health and the health and well-being of plants, animals and other people around us.

But the work that had the greatest impact was "Spiritual Emergency" by Stanislav and Christina Grof (a husband and wife team – very interesting!). This book provided me with a language that made sense of my own earlier experiences.

Right at the start of their book Stanislav and Christina set out a very new and different way of looking at the dramatic experiences and unusual states of mind that people can go through at times in their lives. These are what traditional psychiatry usually diagnoses and treats as a "mental illness". Hearing voices in your head and seeing visions, for example, are not just "psychoses", but, according to Stanislav and Christina, signs that someone is going through a transformation, both personal and spiritual.

That's why they come up with the term "spiritual emergency" to describe these experiences. I think it's a great phrase because it connects two meanings; the idea of both a crisis and an opportunity for someone to break through to a new level of awareness, and personal transformation. In short, an emergence of the spiritual self.

∽

From this insight the Grofs went on to develop a whole new way of understanding and assisting people through what they have termed "transformative states".

What is a "transformative state" I hear you say? Stanislav and Christina explain how most of the time we experience ourselves in the here and now, as physical beings living in a material world. Using our five senses we see only what is happening in our immediate surroundings and at that particular time.

When we go into a "transformative" state of mind everything changes. We begin to experience ourself and the world differently and "normal" space and time dissolves. Our many selves start experiencing many different levels of being – we begin to have a multi-dimensional awareness. We experience vividly the energies around us and within us. The boundaries between our own consciousness and separate realities begin to blur and we can experience interconnection with other people around us and with all of humanity (what Carl Jung called the collective consciousness). We can also experience the life force and consciousness of animals, plants, trees, rocks, water.

Interestingly enough what Grof and Grof describe here is in the African, Aboriginal and Native American world view of the natural order of things; the interconnectedness with and connectedness across dimensions. In these ancient wisdom traditions people will talk of entering what is known as "the dream time", or the realm of the ancestors, and of communing with the spirits of animals, water, trees, rocks.

So what Stansilav and Christina wrote linked all sorts of things up for me. I could certainly recognise some of my own experiences in these descriptions, but also began to recognise other people's experiences as well. Maybe you can too.

At this point I had finished my training and was working both as a lecturer in Counselling and as a counsellor working with both men and women but mainly with women. Although not a natural academic, I took the plunge and embarked on a Masters Degree, encouraged by one of my lecturers, Dr William West.

Fate had led me to William, who had a particular interest in spiritual issues in counselling, and has written several fascinating books on this subject. In one of these, entitled "Psychotherapy & Spirituality", he asks the question: "Are counsellors and psychotherapists willing to address the spiritual dimensions of people's lives?" My answer was definitely, "yes!" as I had already made my work on spiritual emergency the focus of my own research.

I started out by interviewing people in depth about their own experiences of seeking help from professional counsellors. What began to emerge, from the life stories many students and clients were telling me, was a pattern, or common thread, which linked back to my own personal "crisis" or awakening.

One common theme was the experience of intense periods of emotional upheaval, which were often interpreted as evidence of mental instability by friends, family and doctors and frequently led to psychiatric medicines being prescribed.

For many of the people I talked to these episodes were not just painful and frightening, but also involved very positive feelings. People who had previously had no interest found themselves writing beautiful and inspiring pieces of writing and poetry. Some were experiencing nature in a different way and seeing life as they had never seen it before suddenly more beautiful, which filled them with a feeling of well being, connectedness to nature in all her expressions including Angels and Spirit guides.

It was the negative reactions of others that fuelled doubt and fear, leading to self-censorship, and often a decision to fall silent rather than attempt to communicate, even when there was a desperate need to ask questions and share experiences.

The problem of spiritual emergency is not that it happens, but the unsupportive responses of those who are around people going through it.

This in turn creates fear in the person at the centre of the storm, and because these transitions can be challenging by their very nature, the fear of those around reinforces the negative aspects of the experience and diminishes the positive, so that a "dream time" becomes a time of nightmares, and an emergence becomes an emergency.

One of the women I interviewed, who had experienced this very strongly, put it really well:

"Like birth can be made difficult, sometimes it can be

difficult, but sometimes it can be made difficult as well by how you are treated. It kind of has similarities there because it's like being born, different stages".

∽

Just as we have midwives to help women give birth, so we also need midwives to help give birth to aspects of the self.

For thousands of years, in countries across the world, many others have been through similar experiences. In many cultures, they have had many wise guides to help them. So where are the guides for us now, in our modern urban communities?

There are I believe a growing number of people in this culture, some of them professionals, some counsellors, "alternative" therapists, some priests, priestesses, some religious, others spiritual, some just ordinary people who are spiritual in their approach to life, who are trying to provide help and support. But not enough. And in this modern society things are often not made easy for them.

More and more people in this culture at this time need to take responsibility for holding a space for people to give birth to their unique experience of personal enfoldment. The journey can indeed be quite arduous and the path at times can be a lonely and frightening one.

Yet if someone is able to listen, watch, hold, without judgement of what is real or unreal for the person going through this transition, we can be of real help.

This help doesn't have to come from shamans, or healers steeped in ancient lore. It doesn't have to come from professional counsellors or therapists. We can all help, if we are prepared to recognise spirituality in our lives, and the lives of others. Open heartedness and compassion goes a long way.

Through embracing your own inner selves, a new spiritual energy is emerging in you, and you, too, will begin to find ways of supporting those around you.

In you; around you; spiritual emergency is coming out of the shadows in to the light.

CHAPTER TWELVE

The Inner Realms

For those of us who have been through a spiritual emergency there can be a long and arduous task of building enough trust back up to feel that there is nothing wrong with our feelings, our perceptions, our intuitions.

There is such a contradiction in this society when it comes to other ways of seeing, knowing and experiencing this thing we call life. It has been well known that on occasion the police have secretly called in the skills and perceptions of people with psychic ability to help when trying to locate missing persons or to locate a body. But at the same time we are told that these things are nothing more than mumbo jumbo and people who experience other or deeper ways of seeing are some how less mentally stable, less intelligent and, worst of all, gullible people.

It's little wonder that the person who has begun to recognise ways of seeing and being beyond the five senses has a tough old time! When we are truly connecting with ourselves spiritually a whole host of emotional stuff gets thrown up to be worked on and healed.

This can be particularly difficult if you are the sort of person who does not like to connect emotionally, perhaps because you believe that to allow yourself to connect emotionally is weak or "primitive."

An emotional overload can be triggered by anything, from the loss of someone through death or the break up of a relationship, or even getting in touch with feelings through true love making. If you are used to suppressing your emotional self, this can be a difficult, frightening experience.

But this is not the time to panic and seek to numb our feelings by recourse to tablets, pills, alcohol, drugs, base charka sex, or any other disconnecting substances.

Staying separate from our emotions keeps us away and separate from the spiritual centre of our being. The emotions are the natural inner guides of our spiritual self.

Let us allow ourselves to experience the spiritual from the inside, from the deep inner reaches of our self.

From the womb of our self.

Quite often when people are at their lowest they find themselves in the foetus position to console themselves. In the foetus position we are trying to reconnect to that divine energy, when we are emotionally upset, hurt or simply drunk.

In a spiritual or emotional crisis people - both male and female - adopt the foetus position quite naturally; it is an inbuilt response that we come with. Nobody teaches us that this is the position to adopt in times of crisis. We just know. It is a birthing position.

Quite often our spiritual journey of healing is entwined with themes of life, death & birth. Not just birth but the nature of rebirth.

Our emotional turmoil is the struggle of rebirth.

Once we have started on the journey, we can begin to help others who wish to join us. But this, too, is a struggle.

What is desperately needed by people or souls in crisis is birthing partners, midwives and enablers of both genders.

Are we prepared to be a birthing partner to others? Are we prepared to travel the dimensions of our birthing partners to places and terrains akin to a journey through the underworld of the person?

At times working with someone is like accompanying them on a shamanic journey.

There may be times when dark energy entities have been hovering around us, and there will be times when you can feel the sacredness of the presence of the creator close by, in the centre of you and your companion.

This I believe to be the third presence people have reported touching and experiencing in therapy. I name this and call this the sacred trinity of being.

We have reached the sacred place of birthing new aspects and dimensions of self yet unknown.

The good news is that, just as we can generate negative energy through making the wrong choices, we can alter our energy vibrations in a positive and healing way by making some good choices.

We can do this right now, in the alchemy of this moment that is the birth of the rest of our life.

We do not have to disconnect our heart from our head.

We do not have to neglect and abuse the natural world around us.

We do not have to mess up our minds and spirits through over-indulgence in alcohol or drugs or abusive sexual relationships.

We do not have to punish ourselves forever as "sinners", but can choose to forgive ourselves now in this instant.

In fact, we carry within us all the resources we need to nurture and grow ourselves and the world we live in. We just need to connect to what is within us.

We need to reach the sacred space within us.

No matter what our journey to get there, whether our gateway in is through opening ourselves to meditation, ritual, giving birth, an intense sexual encounter, religion or prayer, or whether it is in reaction to the dangers of drugs, alcohol, addictions, the split of a relationship, an illness, a prison sentence, there are many, many gateways into the universe within, gateways that open the dimensions that are interconnected with the inner universe and the universe of stars and galaxies.

Yes, there are those who want us to stay trapped here. Well, maybe those are the people we have grown differently from and no longer need to walk beside.

Maybe our paths will be woven together later, may be they won't. Maybe we will just part company and stay on different paths. It is our journey, not theirs. It is time to get rid of the clutter in our lives and sometimes that clutter can include other people and their unhelpful energy. Is it time for you to declutter?

Perhaps most important, maybe you recognise something of yourself in the victims or vampires I have described. If that is the case this might just be a good time for you to seek some spiritual or therapeutic support to help you heal.

If that is too difficult for you right now, remember this: the hardest thing is to see yourself as you are, not the mask you present yourself to be.

So, congratulations! You have given yourself the best chance ever: you have told the truth about yourself to the most important person on the planet – you.

Having the courage to allow yourself to see yourself as you are, maybe for the first time, is a gift. It is not something to give your self a hard time over or to feel guilty about. We all of us on this planet have things we need to heal, and you and I are no exception.

By the way if you do decide to see a therapist, and they tell you or give you the impression that they have worked on all their issues and that they are all sorted - run like hell!

Because none of us have it sorted; I don't care how holy they are or what title they have - priest, priestess, chief - or how many ascended masters they are channelling!

We as human beings are all subject to some form of dysfunctional life experience. Is that not the reason any of us found our way into healing work? Those that profess not to have been subject to any hardship in life must be living on a different planet to the rest of us!

It could be that rather than seeking help for yourself you can begin the healing process by working with others. Having recognised the cycle of abuse in your own life you may find yourself working with others in order to heal yourself. After all, we are all the same family, regardless of where we start the healing process.

You never know, the person you help to see through their time of darkness might be the person who will help heal your family trauma.

It does not really matter where we start our healing journey as long as we start.

Maybe you are going to be one of the world's greatest healers, but just need to free your creative energy from the grip of the unproductive cycle you are in at this time? I don't know. But what I do know is that your potential is always there, no matter how young or old you are. You can always make a difference to someone's life, namely yours!

You can rebirth yourself creatively and energetically and create your own future right now, in this moment in time. Don't take my word for it: test it out for yourself. Watch and listen carefully and you will clearly see and hear the dynamics of a new situation taking shape. Not only will you notice the dynamic change, but if you tune in you will feel it at an energy level.

Try this tiny little exercise

Close your eyes.

Feel this energy now and dare to dream.

How would you like to be? What would you love to do?

See yourself as that or just get a sense of how that would feel.

Breathe in your future you and breathe out your past you with healing forgiveness and blessings.

Now imagine yourself as you would like to be. When you have a strong sense of that person open your eyes and work towards becoming that person.

It's time to detach yourself from the negative thought form that is feeding on your self-victimisation and your blaming energy.

Healing the little hurts.

Think of someone in your adult life who comes to mind who has upset you or hurt your feelings recently.

Now close your eyes and picture them. Don't worry if

you can't picture them - just get a sense of, or imagine the person.

Bring to mind a time when that person did something positive for you.

Now you are in this energy space, allow yourself to connect, with the intention of seeing and truly feeling the goodness in the person... think of a time when that person made you laugh, smile, feel good, helped you out, did something for you.

Just stay in that energy for a little while and really allow your spirit to experience the goodness in the other person.

Now from the place you are in right now at this moment ask yourself this question: did that person deliberately set out to hurt you, or is it possible they just did the wrong thing but for the right reasons? Were they just human beings doing the best they could with the knowledge and understanding they had at that time?

It's time to grow and heal, stop blaming and victimising and embrace your compassion.

People did make mistakes with you and some times those mistakes hurt you. But you know what? Those past mistakes don't have to keep hurting you. You have the power and the grace to see them for what they were: dysfunctional mistakes and inadequate parenting, friendship and human error.

You have the power to let go of them and see the people who made those mistakes for what they were - emotionally frightened children trying to do the best they could with the knowledge and understanding they had at that particular time, sometimes with very little support, or knowledge.

It's time for you now to focus on not what was said or done to you, but to focus on the question: how can I heal from this? What were the gifts in this? How did this add to my character? What in this has made me stronger?

When you are done thank the person for their kindness and their goodness. Thank yourself for being gracious and courageous enough to see the good in the person.

If you can't yet find it in your heart to thank this person, don't worry. Depending on how great the hurt this person caused you, it may take time. You should still thank yourself for having the courage to go back and look again at such a painful part of your life, and for reaching out to find the healing beyond the hurt. You might even be at a place in your life right now where counselling might be helpful.

Be grateful, for it is this ability to see beyond the story of your life that will carry you through to creating the life you want.

And let us remember once again at all times to keep true to our intent to do the right thing.

If we worshiped the sacredness we carry in ourselves a fraction of the amount we worship things outside ourselves we would have the intention of connecting to that sacred aspect that lives inside us.

Now wouldn't that be something? To recognise the sacredness of self would mean we would stop setting other people up to hurt us and stop setting others up to hurt them.

We would stop damaging and disrespecting the natural world.

If we could recognise the sacredness in self and the

interconnectedness of others it would mean having an interconnected responsibility on a psycho-spiritual level. We would realise that those we worship are no more worthy or special or sacred than you or I, they have just realised their potential to be in touch with that which lives in all of us.

Each one of us is just as sacred and as knowing and contains just as much wisdom as those we put on a pedestal.

What you have to do is to place some of that projected sacredness back inside yourself. You are worthy and can make a difference; you just have to believe you can.

You are entitled to have your own intent, to follow your own path. What you learn and how you learn it may be different from your friends, family members or group of people you are in relationship with right now.

You are entitled to reach your own sacred centre in your own footsteps in response to healing that you need to do for your own, your very own, personal dysfunction and understanding.

It's what I call soul alchemy.

There is usually a very special place in the sacred journey to acceptance of the self.

Not the self we pretend to be so others will like us, no: the sacred stripped bare self that we are birthed into.

When we touch that sacred space where we truly meet self, that place within that brings us to our knees with the truth of who we are.

Where we first meet ourselves as we really are and we are filled with the sheer knowledge of the vastness of who we are, including the inner shadow that lives within us.

Whatever aspect of yourself you meet behind the

mask of who you present yourself to be in public, one thing is guaranteed: you will never leave this place you have touched within yourself and be the same again.

If you can, this is a good moment to spend some time appreciating your self.

Another little Exercise

Sit quietly in a space where you won't be disturbed. You will need about half an hour of time dedicated just to yourself.

You can if you wish burn incense of your choice; I use different ones depending what my intent is, but you can use any that you feel drawn to.

You can also, if you wish, light a candle and have some relaxation music playing gently in the background. (Sometimes people ask me what I would recommend, but again this is something of a personal choice and you will just have to listen to different ones and decide for yourself which feels and sounds most compatible for you.)

Gently close your eyes and take a few slow deep breaths, breathing in peace and breathing out stress.

Gently feel the relaxation moving up from your toes through to your feet and gently moving up your calves and up through your knees into the deep muscle tissue in your legs, just washing through all that tired muscle and filling you with peace and relaxation.

Allow this peace to move throughout your whole body, resting for a few seconds in your heart centre where you acknowledge and thank your heart for the job it does of being the drumbeat that connects you to the rhythm of life.

Now allow this beautiful energy to move up through the rest of your body feeling your face gently relax, as you unclench your teeth and allow your jaw to relax, and allow the feeling to gently move through your face, bathing your eyelids in peaceful relaxation.

And as the clear peaceful relaxation gently washes through your crown chakra at the top of your head imagine, feel, see, or just get a sense of a beautiful delicate cascade of white light gently bathing your crown chakra and washing through your whole body, filling you with a sense of warmth as if you are being wrapped in a soft blanket of unconditional love and acceptance.

Feel that inner glow all through your body. Get a sense and a feeling of perfect peace that fills your being with the unconditional self love that is the very core of who you are.

Just allow yourself to bask in this energy for as long as you need to allow yourself to drink in this beautiful energy that is the essence of the goodness of your spirit.

When you feel ready, slowly and gradually bring yourself back into the here and now.

Feel yourself strong and grounded in this present moment.

In the strength and beauty of spirit that is you.

CHAPTER THIRTEEN

The End, Or the Beginning

So, you've turned to the final pages and it's now time for you to do one more thing.

It's time to go back to the first step you took as you began your journey through this little book.

Okay, sit - or stand if you prefer - and take three deep breaths. Breathe in slowly and breathe out slowly… good.

Now, ask yourself honestly, is your life truly what you would want for yourself?

Are you happy? Are you hurting?

Do you feel you are heading in the right direction?

Close your eyes for a minute or two and just think about the answers to these questions.

If you can, think back to the answers you gave when you started the book.

If you wrote anything down, this is the time to read back through your jottings.

What if anything has changed in the time between then and now?

What if anything is the difference between you-then and you-now?

What has grown in you, and what are you now ready to cast aside?

And what are you going to do now?

Don't rush; there's plenty of time to make the changes in your life that would benefit you and the ones you love.

For the time being, get to know your sacred self.

Look after your natural self by making sure that what you put in and around your body makes it feel healthier and stronger.

Look after your sexual self by avoiding abusive partners and seeking loving companions.

Look after your cultural self by talking to your elders more and learning about your ancestors.

Let your political self lead by example, and empower others.

I hope you have found your journey through this book of some help to you in facing your life's challenges, and in embracing the potential of your whole self.

After all, your journey is also part of mine.

It's all about you, me and us.

Love, Light and Blessings.

Printed in the United Kingdom
by Lightning Source UK Ltd.
131988UK00001B/79-117/A